EARLY HISTORY

OF

HOPKINS COUNTY

TEXAS

BIOGRAPHICAL SKETCHES AND INCIDENTS
OF THE EARLY SETTLED FAMILIES

BY

E. B. FLEMING

Southern Historical Press, Inc.
Greenville, South Carolina

SOUTHERN HISTORICAL PRESS, INC.
PO BOX 1267
Greenville, SC   29601

ISBN #0-89308-186-8

Printed in the United States of America

DEDICATION.

TO THE COMING
GENERATION, TO THE
BOYS AND GIRLS, TO THE PIONEER
CITIZEN AND OLD SOLDIER OF HOPKINS
COUNTY, TEXAS. TO MY DEAR DAUGHTER, MRS. MABEL
MOORE, I DEDICATE THIS BOOK
AS A TRIBUTE OF AFFECTION,
LOVE AND ESTEEM.

E. B. F.

PREFACE.

Every one prizes a book that puts much in a small space. Within the pages of this book will be found a vast collection of important facts relating to biography, genealogy and historical incidents stored with useful information, while at the same time it is full of entertainment for all readers. But little attention has been paid to the preservation of biography except in so far as it pertained to the preferred class. There is a growing demand from the common people—the popular class—for the preservation not only of biography, but of family genealogy; not for its immediate worth, but for its future value and a laudable pride in its perpetuation for the rising and coming generation; the difficulty experienced in gathering the material for this book forcibly illustrates the necessity for work of this character. In many cases it is found that nearly all reliable trace of ancestry is lost back of the father.

No pains have been spared to make the facts to be found within the book accurate.

To those who have rendered assistance by furnishing facts and material, we tender our acknowledgments.

THE AUTHOR.

INTRODUCTION.

The city of Sulphur Springs contains about 5000 souls. It is beautifully situated on the divide between the timber lands and prairie lands, with a good supply of wood and water for all purposes. Every religious denomination is represented by large commodious church buildings, with a large church membership and some of the ablest divines in the State of Texas. We have as fine legal talent and as forceful bar as is in the state, with many industrial enterprises at a great cost. Fine schools and a healthy city. The moral tone of the town is exceptionally good. With good city and county officials to enforce the law. Two large National Banks that do a big business annually. The merchants and business men of the town are all honest, upright and just men, enjoying the full confidence of the trading public and do a large amount of business yearly. We have electric lights, water works and the best sewerage system in the state. The town is in a healthy, growing and prosperous condition.

TABLE OF CONTENTS.

SULPHUR SPRINGS DIRECTORY.

The people whose names are listed in this directory are **the** substantial business men of the city, and merit the full confidence of the public. The professional men are those upon whom the people can rely with perfect safety.

J. A. STEVENSON IMPLEMENT COMPANY.
Dealer in Moline Farm Implements, Peter Shuttler Wagons, Barb Wire and other staple hardware. Agent for McCormick Machinery, and J. I. Case Thresher.

C. L. MURRIE & COMPANY.
Dealers in Dry Goods, Millinery, Ladies' Furnishings. The only up-to-date Store of this kind in the city.

O. M. PATE.
Dealer in Hardware, Stoves, Sash and Doors, Furniture, etc., in fact in everything to build and furnish a house.

GEO. A. WILSON.
Manufacturer of Compressed brick the most substantial Builder and Contractor in North East Texas.

JNO. D. WILLIAMS.
Dealer in Saddles, Harness, Buggies and Bicycles. Of twenty years standing.

B. F. ASHCROFT & SONS.
Proprietors of Sulphur Springs Electric Light Plant and Big Four Gin. Thirty-two years standing.

W. W. WILLIAMSON.
Dealer in Fancy and Staple Groceries. The only up-to-date Grocery in the city.

W. A. SMITH.
W. A. Smith, "The Land Man," Buys and Sells More Land than any other man in Texas. He is Notary Public.

H. E. HENDERSON.
Dealer in Dry Goods and Fancy Groceries. Bargains in every line of Reliable Dry Goods, a first-class house for Planters' Supplies.

FRANK E. YANTIS.
Dealer in Watches, Clocks and Jewelry. Keeps in stock a full supply of the best that money will buy from manufacturer.

T. K. PROCTOR, M. D.
Specialist in Ear, Eye, Nose and Throat. Chronic diseases and all forms of the Drug habit.

V. M. CLARK.
Attorney at Law, Kellogg Building.

CROSBY & DINSMORE.
Attorneys and Counselors at Law.

J. C. STAFFORD.
The Meat Man.

J. M. MELSON.
Attorney at Law. Collecting Agent.

THE FIRST NATIONAL BANK.
M. De Loach, President; E. E. Tomlinson, Vice-President; Phil H. Foscue, Cashier. Capital and Surplus, $150,000.00. Sulphur Springs, Texas.

J. F. CARTER.
The old pioneer Grocer of Sulphur Springs. Come and see me for honest, reliable goods.

R. N. SELLERS.
Dealer of Staple and Fancy Groceries. West of D. M. Smith & Co.

PARIS GROCER COMPANY.
Wholesale Grocers. Sulphur Springs, Texas.

SHOE TALK.
Are you satisfied with the shoes you have been buying? Are they what they should be? Good shoes cost less than poor ones. I guarantee every pair of my shoes—T. P. Kirkpatrick, South Side Connally Street, Sulphur Springs, Texas.

THE CITY NATIONAL BANK.
W. O. Womack, President; S. D. Greaves, Vice-President; J. F. Carter, Vice-President; W. F. Skillman, Cashier; W. W. Jones, Assistant Cashier. Capital and surplus, $150,000.00. Sulphur Springs, Texas.

R. D. ALLEN.
District Attorney 8th Judicial District. General Practitioner.

T. S. CHRISTIAN & CO.
Clothiers and Gents' Furnishers, Boots, Shoes, Hats, etc.

J. M. PIERSON.
Dealer in Pianos, Organs and Sewing Machines. Of more than twenty years standing, high grade goods and low prices.

JNO. D. RAY.
Manufacturer of Saddlery and Harness. Dealer in Buggies and Bicycles. Proprietor of the Sulphur Springs Tannery. Bring me your Hides and Bark.

WILBER STANLEY.
Dealer in Dry Goods, Notions and Shoes.

If you are in need of Good Fresh Groceries, see
GEO. R. YANTIS. Feed stuff a specialty.

A. B. ELLIS.
Merchant Tailor. Cleaning and repairing neatly done. South side of the Square, Johnson Building, Upstairs.

PERKINS DRY GOODS COMPANY.
Dry Goods, Clothing, Shoes, Hats and Gents' Furnishing Goods. One Price, Spot Cash, South side of the Square, Yesner Building.

W. H. DICKERSON.
Tax Collector of Hopkins County.

J. M. COLQUITT.
The Oldest Dry Goods Dealer in the city. Up-to-date Goods, Honest Values, and Low Prices. First-Class Grocery Department in rear of Building.

P. W. TEMPLETON.
Dealer in Family Groceries. A First-Class House for the buyer. Honest, just dealings and satisfaction guaranteed.

J. B. DAVIS.
Leader in Groceries, Feed Stuff and Country Produce. Call me up when you want me.

CARGILE BROS.
The Grocers are looking after the best city trade. We keep the freshest line of Groceries and the best quality at all times.

C. W. HIGGINS.
Dry Goods, Notions, Gents' Furnishings; want your chickens and eggs.

DENTAL PARLORS.
My methods are those practiced in the largest cities of to-day. Plate, Crown and Bridge work a specialty, dentistry in all its branches, parlors in Robertson Building.

MILLER & MILLER.
Hardware.

W. C. HURLEY.
Postmaster.

M. BOYD.
Dealer in Drugs and Sundries.

J. A. HURLEY.
Attorney at Law.   Kellogg Building.

ASKEW & BUFORD.
Dealers in Drugs, Medicines, Paints, Oils, etc.

T. C. McCORKLE.
Manager of the Alliance Cotton Yard.   This institution under his management has been a great success.

W. M. WALKER.
Dealer in Drugs, Toilet Articles, Paints and Oils.

J. B. ASKEW & CO.
Dealers in Staple and Fancy Groceries, also the Famous New Harrison Wagon.

B. W. FOSTER.
Attorney at Law.

THORNTON & SWEETON.
Attorneys and Counselors at Law.

GEO. A. BERGIN.
Dealer in Fine Monuments.

W. I. IRWIN.
Dealer in Meats and Cattle.

COTTER & McMULLEN.
Dealers in Family Groceries and Bakery.   The oldest Grocery firm in the city.

LIVERY AND TRANSFER COMPANY.
P. Z. Littlefield Proprietor and Joe Littlefield Manager.

RAYMOND DIAL MERCANTILE COMPANY.
At the Famous Mississippi Store.

FRANK E. SCOTT.
Attorney at Law. Land Bought and Sold.

DIAL & DIAL.
Physicians and Surgeons.

J. R. FERGUSON.
Justice of the Peace, Precinct No. 1.

I. M. DAWSON.
Dealer in Family and Fancy Groceries and all kinds of Produce, best equipped Wagon Yard in the city.

THEO WIEGERS.
Dealer in Hardware.

BEN E. SMITH.
Carries the largest line of Drugs, Jewelry, Watches, Diamonds, Silverware and Cut Glass. Our prices will interest the prospective buyer. Call and see us.

M. G. MILLER.
Dealer in Staple and Fancy Groceries.

D. M. SMITH & CO.
Dealers in Hardware.

ROBERT S. BLYTHE.
Attorney and Counselor at Law.

W. P. LEACH.
Attorney and Counselor at Law.

C. O. JAMES.
Attorney at Law.

R. B. KEASLER.
County Judge and Attorney at Law.

W. C. STIRLING, M. D.
Specialist of Eye, Ear, Nose and Throat. Chronic diseases of all kinds treated.

D. B. BIRTHRIGHT.
Dealer in General Merchandise.

FRANK A. WHITE, B. LIT., M. D.
Physician and Surgeon.

KING & BIRD.
Dealers in Dry Goods, Clothing, Boots, Shoes, Hats and Caps; in fact in everything kept in a First-Class Store. Call and see us.

M. MOELK.

Established in 1880. Has sold honest Boots and Shoes for twenty-two years in the city of Sulphur Springs. Call and see me on North side of Main Street.

H. P. ACKER.

Dealer in Staple and Fancy Groceries, Cotton and Country Produce a specialty. Northeast corner of Public Square.

W. T. MOREHEAD.

"The Jeweler."

NELTA DIRECTORY.

J. M. SIMMS. M. D.

Physician and Surgeon.

WILBER J. DAVIS.

Postmaster and Dealer in General Merchandise.

CHAS. B. KIRKBRIDE.

Blacksmith and woodwork. Bois'D'Arc Wagons a specialty.

WARRICK FRANCE.

The only Gin man in the place.

CHAPTER I.

Government has existed since the birth of man. Opinions differ with people and with nations as to the goal to be reached by this or by that method, but the intelligent person watches with interest the growth in any form of the great science of politics and government.

Some countries still think the individual exists for the benefit of the government rather than the government for the governed. It is not the intention of the author to write a treatise on the science of government, or a history of the great State of Texas; But it has been suggested and thought advisable to speak of the manner by which the Americans came into the possession of the territory of the State of Texas. This vast territory once belonged to Mexico, at the time of Moses Austin's visit to Texas, the Mexican government had just passed through a bloody revolution. Moses Austin, a Missourian, called upon the Governor at San Antonio and presented his petition to locate a colony on Texas soil. After many disappointments and suffering hardships, his petition was approved. He then returned to his home in Missouri and died.

This grant authorized Austin to settle three hundred families in Texas At Moses Austin's death he requested that his son should take up the work and carry out his father's plans. Stephen F. Austin went to San Antonio in August 1821 and was cordially received by the authorities, who granted young Austin permission to explore the country adjacent to the Colorado River, and choose what lands he wished. Austin selected for his colony the region lying south of the San Antonio road, between the San Jacinto and Lavaca rivers. This included some of the most fertile land in the province. Austin returned to his home and advertised for Colonists, to each man over twenty-one he promised six hundred and forty acres of land. If a married man he received nine hundred and sixty acres, each child brought its father one hundred and sixty acres, while each slave brought his master eighty acres. When a colonist erected a mill or a store house he was given more land. All immigrants were to be free from taxation for six years. All colonists were required to become Roman Catholics. At this time Spain laid claim to Texas territory. A war soon occurred between the Republic of Mexico and Spain. On account of this revolution in Mexico, Austin was compelled to go to the City of Mexico and have his grant renewed. It required twelve months time for Austin to succeed in having his grant renewed. He returned to his colony to find many of them gone. Discouraged by his long absence Baron de Bastrop was appointed to survey lands and with the help of Austin to issue to the colonists land deeds in the name of the Mexican

government. In 1825 Austin completed his contract with the government having introduced the
three hundred families called for in his contract.
Austin then asked for and obtained permission
to bring in five hundred families more; other men
obtained permits and brought colonists into Texas.
In 1828 the Mexican government wisely threw open
to settlers the ten leagues of coast lands and twenty
leagues of border lands that had been kept for
government use. Texas was interspersed with American colonists and waste places were fast giving
way to fertile fields, blooming gardens and flowering
yards.

Texas was until 1824 a separate province of
Mexico, but at that time Texas was joined to
Coahulla and the two provinces were changed into
the State of Coahulla and Texas with the capital
located at Saltillo. The whole plan of union with
Coahulla was unpleasant to the Texans. The
Indians were for many years a constant source of
trouble to all Texas colonists. In the year of 1820
there were not more than 4000 civilized inhabitants
in Texas. While in the year of 1830 the state
boasted of 20,000 Americans alone. These Americans, dear reader, were not wild adventurers, but
home seekers who came upon Texas soil to live and
die in the land and home of their adoption. They
had come from every part of the United States.
Texas was at this period under liberal colonization
laws, making rapid strides of progress but a change
was now to come. In the year of 1830 Anastasio

Bustamente, a narrow minded tyrannical military officer, became president of Mexico. One of his first acts was to issue an order prohibiting inhabitants of the United States from settling in Texas. All other nations were cordially invited and heartily welcomed. By the order of this tyrant, Americans were not even permitted to trade in Texas. A great number of the colonists had relatives and friends in the United States who were desirous of joining them in Texas, who had sold their lands in the old states, and many of them were at this time on their way to Texas. The news of this decree spread gloom and sadness over all sections of the state. In 1833 laws were passed by the Mexican Congress relative to the settling in Texas colonies of convicts and deserters, the worst element of citizenship on earth. Therefore it is not strange that our forefathers bitterly objected to these laws. The Mexican laws became very oppressive, in fact distressing and unbearable. To collect the taxes and to see that the laws were obeyed, several bodies of Mexican troops were sent into Texas. Three hundred and fifty Mexican soldiers were stationed at Nacogdoches; one hundred and fifty soldiers at Galveston Bay; the garrisons at both Goliad and San Antonio were increased. The Mexican officials became more and more oppressive and insulting to men and to women alike and the officials began to arrest and to imprison some of the most prominent Americans.

Travis, Allen and others were arrested. They

were imprisoned in the fort and treated as common criminals. The Texans demanded the release of these men. The authorities positively refused to release the prisoners.

In 1832 the colonists held a famous mass meeting, and entered into resolutions. Arms were at once resorted to, and John Austin placed in command. The first battle was fought at Velasco in which the Texans were victorious. No humane reader can find justice in Mexico's rule of Texas. The United States tried to buy Texas from Mexico, and offered four million dollars for the section east of the line dividing the waters of the Rio Grande and the Nueces; this proposition was refused. Mexico was vastly mistaken in the material out of which the Americans were made, and the nature of the men she wished to govern. The Texans now began to prepare for war in dead earnest. Appeal after appeal, all of which were ignored by the Mexican government, had been made by the Texans to repeal the obnoxious and oppressive laws. A committee with Sam Houston as chairman, drew up the Constitution for Texas. In many respects it resembles the Constitution of the United States. In the meantime Santa Anna had, through intrigue and base deception, become dictator of the Republic of Mexico. He soon discovered that Texas was not disposed to yield to his dictation. He therefore determined to crush the Texans into submission. Santa Anna sent his brother-in-law General Cos to Texas with several hundred troops. General Cos proclaimed his mission on every hill. He entended to over run Texas and subdue her citizens and drive out all Americans who came to Texas since 1830. All this time Austin had been in a Mexican dungeon. The Texans replied that with God's help Gen. Cos should find that American freemen would never submit to such tyranny. There was a small brass cannon at Gonzales. The Mexicans demanded the surrender of the cannon. The Texans refused and battle ensued in which the Mexicans were defeated. Goliad was next captured. When Santa Anna learned that Gen. Cos had surrendered at San Antonio he grew desperate and wild with rage. Every reader is conversant with the Massacre at San Antonio. It was here at San Antonio that Gen. Cos had received so disgraceful a defeat. In consequence therefore of this great disaster to the Mexicans, Santa Anna resolved to strike his first blow for vengeance. There were in the garrison at the Alamo 182 men; Travis, Bowie, Crockett and Bonham were in the Alamo, four names that will live forever. Every true Texan is proud of these names, they have gone down in history honored and beloved by their countrymen. The Alamo was captured. Death and Santa Anna were in possession of the historic Alamo. By his orders the bodies of the brave Texans were collected in a large pile and burned. From this most despicable act, from that sacred fire emanated the flames that lighted all Texas that consumed thousands of Mexican lives and humiliated and degraded Santa

Anna and confined him in chains.   In March a con-
vention assembled on the Brazos at Washington
and declared Texas a free and independent republic.
The battle of San Jacinto ended the war and Texas
became an independent republic.   Santa Anna was
captured, carried before Gen. Sam Houston, who re-
primanded him for his cruelty at the Alamo, Santa
Anna replied: "I was acting under the orders of my
government."   Houston said: "You were the government of Mexico; a dictator, sir, has no superiors."
At the entrance to the old capitol at Austin stood a
monument built from the ruins of the Alamo and
dedicated to the heroes who perished there.   The
names of Bowie, Travis, Crockett and Bonham
stood out in bold relief, one on each side.   The east
front bore this inscription: "Thermopylae had her
messenger of defeat; the Alamo had none."   This
is a correct and a condensed account of the manner
by which the Americans came into possession of
Texas the "Lone Star State."

CHAPTER II.

Some one has said that if a man would be happy he must live in harmony with his environments. But in view of the marvelous changes which have taken places during the last fifty years in the county it would appear that the person who seeks happiness according to such reasoning, would have a hard race to keep up with his environments. When one looks back over the time that has intervened between fifty years ago and the present, and compares the then with the now he sees the wonderful changes time has wrought. Then we had a log cabin for court-house, rail pen for grand jurors, split logs for seats for petit jurors and spectators. The first election was held in the brush. A few log cabins in which school was taught with a few plainly dressed, barefooted children, such books as were brought from the States by the pioneer settler. None others could be had. The settler had gold and silver, but suitable books could not be bought. This and many other reason is why the children of the pioneer citizen was not educated. No church-houses were to be seen. Preachers would sometimes come into the county. They were invariably invited, yea even persuaded to stop over and preach for a people hungry for the gospel. They passed over the country on horse back, perhaps a mustang, with saddle bags, Bible in one end and shirt in the other. They were given a cordial welcome, a kind reception, a hearty greeting among the pioneer settlers. The preacher of that day had a great deal to contend with. The people who moved to this county at that time did not come as a rule to seek religion. The dignified, elegantly dressed pastor of to-day, with his fluent speech and polished manner would doubtless have felt that he was a harbinger of refinement "crying in the wilderness of barbarism." He may have been a thing of beauty but certainly not a "joy forever." It is claimed that professional preachers of to-day are inclined to dictation. In these early times the pastor preached that it was every man's inalienable right as well as his indispensable duty to study the Bible for himself and to formulate his own faith from the teachings of the Bible. The sick and the afflicted, the fatherless and the widow and especially the poor and the needy were visited by neighbors and the preacher. Gold and social influence was not exalted above piety and humble devotion in the church. Their motto was to save the sinners and if needs be let the devil take the church-house. The modern rule is "let the devil take the sinners and save our costly and fashionable church." It is said that the first lumber, real sawed lumber, that was ever had in Hopkins County was sawed by a Mr. Jordan and son, on White Oak Creek, near the Clark crossing. It took several men to operate this primitive machine for the manufacture of lumber. The log was hewed to a square with a broad axe and then lined on the upper and lower sides at every place where it was to be sawed. The people of that day had faults of course, but greed and avarice was not of them. Greed is the most pitiful passion that ever cursed mankind. This passion will induce those who are afflicted with the curse to endeavor to rent heaven out to be used as a pasture if, by so doing, they could make it profitable to themselves. Everybody was content to enjoy what few blessings they had without a desire to monopolize the world. Homesteads could be obtained by pre-emption, 320 acres to the head of a family, 80 acres to a single man. Men occupied government land in many places in the county for years without a shadow of legal title to it. Every neighbor knew that the only right they had to it was that they had selected it and built a house and cleared a farm on it. It was generally understood that anybody could file a legal claim upon such tracts of land at the government land office, and take them from the claimants with all the improvements belonging to them, and, yet, strange as it may appear to the two legged razor backs, such settlers were never molested. There was simply less greed for gain then than now. In that day of honesty, people had not learned to make a display of wealth. The richest people could only use what they could eat and wear, and the poor classes could easily gather that much from nature's bountiful supply by a little work. The old pioneer settler will endorse the author when he says, that day was an age of sociability, equality, hospitality and general neighborliness. Brother! Our dependence upon one another drew us close together. House-raising, log-rollings and corn-shucking among the men, and quilting among the women, often called the entire neighborhood together for a day of work and social pleasure. The wife would invite her lady friends to a quilting, the same day the husband called his neighbor men to assist him at a log-rolling. While men and boys rolled logs, women and girls cooked and quilted, and all united in a big frolic at night. People married then as they do now. On Sulphur creek a Mr. R. married. He and his bride were members of good respectable families. Before the celebration of the marriage he leased a piece of land from Mr. H. which he agreed to clear and fence for the privilege of cultivating it for five years. He built a log cabin in which he proposed to go to housekeeping with the help of his prospective bride. When their fortunes were united, they took an inventory of their available assets, which consisted of one old ox, a slide and a few articles of household and kitchen furniture which the bride received as bridal presents from her parents. As the bride was both a beauty and a reigning belle, she received many little presents from her acquaintances. The next day after the wedding the old ox was harnessed to the slide and the bride's goods were packed and placed in the slide, a bed, an oven, a skillet, a bucket and half dozen pair of deer hams, and a part of a side of hog meat, a gourd of lard and a gourd of sugar completed the inventory. The bride and the groom took a seat on top, of the load and with a gee-buck, and a hearty good-bye to their parents, started on a short bridal tour to the cabin in Sulphur bottom. In that day, some fifty years ago, there was nothing unusual about this bridal tour and whatever amusement it may excite now serves only to emphasize the changes that have taken place in the customs of the county since that time. Emigrants to the county in this early day settled near and convenient to timber and water. Houses were all built of logs. Then the logs were cut and hauled to the place where the house was wanted, the neighbors were requested to come together on a set day and put up the building. This was called a house-raising. These logs were drawn by oxen, with the use of log chains, to the place of building. The house was always built in one day. The walls raised, floor laid often out of puncheons, and roof put on. The finishing touches, stopping the cracks, building the chimney and putting down the hearth were left for the owner to attend to in his own way and at such times as suited his convenience. It was no unusual thing to leave but the sleepers and use the ground for a floor. In fact when a man was able to have two houses, the one used for a kitchen and dining room almost invariably had a dirt floor. The old puncheon floors were neither air tight nor ornamental. The edges of each puncheon were hewed to a line with a broad axe, and when the cracks between them did not measure over an inch in width at any place the floor was considered good enough. Hens usually made their nests under the cabin floor, possibly to be safe from the intrusion of hawks, owls, minks, foxes and other enemies, and the ease with which the puncheon could be raised was a great convenience in getting eggs. It was almost an impossibility to obtain nails. The cracks between the logs in the walls of the cabin were "chinked" with small pieces of wood split for the purpose and daubed with mud made from red clay and plastered by hand. The process of "daubing" was quite simple. A man stood near the crack and threw the soft mud against the "chink" by handfuls with sufficient force to make it stick fast. The roof of every house was made of clapboards. In the absence of nails the boards were put on the roof by means of "ribs," "butting poles," "knees," "end stuff" and "weight poles." Each of these words had a technical meaning in the architecture of that day which cannot be well understood without some knowledge of the construction of log cabins. When conditions changed and nails could be had, knees, weight poles and butting poles were dispensed with and the boards nailed to the ribs. In a few years ribs were supplanted by the more stylish rafters and lathing. The chimney was built of wood and lined with mud made of clay. When the mud was thoroughly dry it was as hard as brick. When obtainable the fire place was lined bottom, back and sides with large flat rock. The top of the fire place in front was simply the first log of the cabin wall above the opening cut for the fire place. A log of unusual size was alway put in the back of the fire place and the rest of the wood was piled about in front. A back log would often last a day and night. When the nights were very cold a fire was kept up all night. The old timer who had built away out on the prairie hauled wood a long distance. No such things as carpets ever entered into the mind of the pioneer. These cabins usually had one door and one window. Water was hauled in kegs and barrels upon slides from the nearest creeks. While these streams did not run except wet or rainy weather, there were always deep holes of water in these dry creeks. Why the citizen did not take advantage of common sense principles, which was accepted by benighted heathen nations who dug wells and built cisterns centuries before our day is a profound mystery to all thinking people.

CHAPTER III.

Away back in the early settlement of Hopkins County some of the hardest work that women and girls had to do was washing and ironing the clothing in which men did such hard work as had to be done in that day. This washing was a weekly task for the women of every household. There were no steam laundries then. There was not even a washing machine or a wringer of any kind. The washing place for a whole neighborhood was a well-shaded spot on the bank of some creek where a clean hole of water could be had. Every girl in the whole neighborhood spent at least one day in each week at the washing place. Sometimes the young men would call around and have a lover's chat with his best girl. This occurrence grew to be common and there was comfort to the heart of every true but modest lover in the thought that she will see her sweetheart on that day. The boys who were too small to work in the field had to help the girls with the washing. The pounding or battling together with their cheerful and merry songs could be heard for a great distance. One old pioneer citizen said to the other: "I often look back to the days I spent with my sisters and my sweetheart under mammoth oak trees in balmy spring, sultry sum-

mer and melancholy autumn as among the happiest
of my life." It was the work of the small boy
to keep the kettles filled with water, brought
from the hole in the creek over the steep and slip-
pery banks, carry wood and keep up the fires and
do most of the battling while the mother or sister
stood over the tub and did the rubbing. No
doubt but that the girls often bent over the wash
tub with a new joy at their hearts, a flush on their
cheeks, a quiver in their breath and unshed tears
of delight and happiness in their eyes because of
the sight of the approach of their lover. Every
house-wife manufactured her own soap. There
was not a pound of soap in the whole country except
that which the women made. All the bones from
the bacon, beef, pork, deer, bear used by the family
during the year, scraps of every kind were care-
fully saved for soap grease. All this made more
work and drudgery for the women. The alkali
used in making soap. Soft soap was obtained from
the ashes which accumulated in those large, old-
time fire-places during the cold season. An "ash-
hopper" was an indispensable article of out-door
furniture in every home. The ashes were put
into the hopper as they accumulated in the fire-
place during the cold season. When the time
came to make soap in the early spring, water had
to be hauled from the creeks or holes in the creek,
however distant the water. The girls who did
the washing, ironing and soap making are the
mothers of some of the most honored, esteemed

and respected citizens of Hopkins County, having imbibed the industrious habits of their mothers they became useful men in the county. The influence of a mother upon her offspring is as lasting as life. By her example and precept homes are made happy or miserable, hence the fearful responsibility that hangs over the mother. The quiltings of long ago deserves a place in these reminiscences. They were simply feminine accomplishments of house raisings and sometimes log rollings. When the men and boys were gathered together to raise a house there the women and girls would be also engaged in a quilting. When the house was raised and the quilting was done the young men and young ladies joined in a midnight revel, dancing, songs and plays common to that day and generation, such as "How lonely is the turtle dove," "Hog drovers we are, etc.," was sung in a hilarious and merry manner. Kissing was a part of all these plays, which was always performed in the presence of the players and singers and not under cover of darkness. The best element of citizens engaged in these pastimes for amusement. Notwithstanding these plays and songs, innocent in their performance, were endorsed by the parents. Religion was far more universally respected than now. In fact everybody believed in it. The author does not remember of hearing of a skeptic or infidel in the whole county as far back as forty-five years ago. Everybody who could get religion was a member of some church, and those who could not get it rarely ceased to try, and never seemed to doubt the reality of heaven and hell, the existence of God and the inspiration of the Bible. In regard to this honest, sincere dealings and actions of the people in that day, we quote the following mental food for the thoughtful reader to ponder over and to digest: "The ecclesiastic history of the world, as well as the plain words of the Savior, seems to indicate rather that the kingdom of heaven cometh not with observation. The ages of spiritual decadence in the history of the church have always been characterized by immense revenues, large endowments, costly houses of worship and glittering paraphernalia. All reformations in religion have succeeded by the personal zeal of poor, penniless advocates against the fat or plethoric purses of richly endowed churches. When religious people depend more upon money than upon morality, more upon collections than upon consecration, more upon policy than upon prayer, more upon vanity than upon virtue, more upon looks than love and more upon fine houses than upon firm faith and pure hearts, the time of their dissolution as a religious body is at hand. Strong churches, fine brick and stone houses and plenty of money, all these may be very well in their way, but without charity they are but "sounding brass or tinkling cymbal."

CHAPTER IV.

When a few old pioneers with their families came into the territory out of which Hopkins County was created there was no postoffice, no mails, no schools, no newspapers, no store houses nearer than Clarksville or the "pin hook" place known as Paris. What corn was used was hauled from the Red River District, bread was obtained by the use of mortar and pestle, no mills for grinding had been erected nearer than forty or fifty miles. The mortar was a small basin hollowed out of a stump or felled tree, mortised so as to have a capacity of half bushel or a peck of corn. The pestle was a smooth piece of hard timber something near the size of the basin in the mortar. This pestle was attached to a lever. This lever was operated by one hand, raising and lowering the pestle upon the corn in the basin. You now have in your mind a clear picture of the meal making machinery in this county fifty-five years ago. When there was a scarcity of corn or when it could not be had at all, the dry meat from the breast of wild turkeys and venison hams, thoroughly dried, made pretty fair substitutes for bread. Some of the old pioneers say that they have used such substitutes for bread weeks at a time and yet they say that life was more enjoyable then than now,

with all of our patent flour and improved cooking.
Meal making was a slow process, of course, but
there was no demand for any great hurry in the
business then. Nobody seemed to have any ambition to get rich or to own the world, and there
was nothing to do but pound the meal in the mortar
and hunt deer and other game common to the
country. Many of these grand old men and women
still live in the simple style of the good times of
old, and it is their delight to talk about the country
and its inhabitants as they knew them in the day
when old hunters flourished in the land. One of
these old pioneers, Uncle Henry Barclay, was
particularly interesting to the author in relating his
varied experiences when a boy in Hopkins County
on Sulphur Creek. He pointed out where he had
stood in his yard and killed a deer. He lives in
a log cabin on the brow of the hill that overlooks
the dense wild wood and forest growth of Sulphur
bottom, a grand old man, who fully realizes that
his race is about run. He settled where he now
lives fifty years ago. He showed the exact spot
where a gray eagle had caught a calf, where the
catamounts had whipped his favorite dog. The
spot where the bear had so frightened his brood
sow that she ran away back to Red River County
where he had got her from. He lives near Uncle
Perry Hargrave, another aged and esteemed old
pioneer citizen who has given the author many
exciting and interesting incidents of his long life
in Hopkins County. He is old now and is suffer-

ing from weakness of age. One of the leading characteristics of those old settlers is their preference for old times. In their style of dress and habits of life they adhere closely to the old ways. One of these old men, Uncle Lodwick Vaden, eighty-three years of age, mounted an old horse and rode, a few days ago, to Sulphur Springs, his county town, and attended to his business and returned to his home none the worse for his ride. The old pioneer hunters often clothed themselves in garments made from the skins of wild beasts. Their fashionable suits consisted of coonskin cap, panther skin vest, buckskin breeches and rawhide foot wear. Any of the old-time settlers in this county will tell you that the wolves howled and the panthers screamed, the wild cat and the catamount cried and the whippoorwill chanted its lonely, solemn and melancholy solo around their lonely cabins in the woods every night. Sheep had to be put in pens surrounded by high picket fences every night, near by their owner's cabin, to save them from the wolves, and many of the settlers kept young calves under their cabin floors at night to protect them from wolves and panthers. Young people of the year 1902 have no idea, not even the most remote, what hardships their forefathers endured in the early settlement of Hopkins County. A Mr. Payne moved into the county and settled in a log cabin on South Sulphur Creek in an early day with his wife and two babies. He was a poor man, and he had to seek employment in order to support

his wife and two infant children till he could get
his own land cleared. There was no one who
could give him employment nearer than twenty-
five miles from his log cabin on Sulphur creek.
He kissed his wife and babies and left home on
Monday, he camped where he had employment
to split rails by the hundred, and boarded himself
and returned to his family on Saturday nights.
This poor man would chop fire wood around his
cabin all day Sunday, carry it on his shoulder
and stack it by his cabin for his wife and children
to burn during the week. He would eat supper
at his humble home Sunday night and walk twenty-
five miles to his camp. By daylight Monday morning he would be at his work, and till late Saturday
night he would work unceasingly from early dawn
till late at night, do his own cooking in his camp,
and sleep by a fire in the woods. And all the time
his wife and two little children were in that lonely
cabin in Sulphur bottom, twenty-five miles away,
with but few neighbors nearer than four miles.
Every night wolves would howl and panthers
scream around her lonely cabin in the woods.
The hooting owl with its strange and peculiar
noise, the lonely, solemn cry of the whippoorwill,
all these things combined was a sufficient cause to
age the wife and turn her hair gray, and frightened
the innocent babies out of their senses. But she
stood it like a heroine, and lives to-day, while her
noble husband is gone to learn the great secret
and wait with the angels in heaven for the coming

of his companion. One of these little children has long since grown to womanhood and is the mother of a large and respectable family in Hopkins County. "Every bitter has its sweet." "There are roses among thorns and a silver lining to every cloud."

CHAPTER V.

There was in an early day in Hopkins County a fine range for all kinds of stock—hogs, horses and cattle. Mast in the timber on the creeks was abundant and hogs gathered a bountiful living in the forest. The branches of forest trees would bend and break under their load of acorns and nuts, and no one pretended to feed hogs only to keep them tame. Every man killed his meat from the woods. The country was peculiarly adapted to the raising of every variety of poultry. All kinds of domestic fowls supported themselves and raised their young by scratching for bugs, and every family was abundantly supplied with eggs and chickens the year round, practically without expense or a great deal of trouble. The greatest and only difficulty in raising poultry was the trouble of protecting the fowls from the ravages of minks, foxes, hawks, owls, pole cats and chicken snakes. Those who craved a stronger beverage than milk at regular meals, contented themselves with tea made from sassafras roots. Persimmon beer was used at the table of many of the early settled families. The ripe persimmons were put in a large keg, warm water was poured on them and left to ferment, when it was ready to serve. Used with baked sweet potatoes it made a nutritious and very strengthening diet. Cows found abundant food in the range the year round, grasses of all kinds grew without stint, the prairie part of Hopkins County afforded the best range for cows. The cane brakes on the creek bottom furnished an inexhaustible supply of excellent provender for them during the winter, and grass grew luxuriantly all over the county during the spring, summer and fall. Every family was therefore abundantly supplied with milk and with butter without any expense at all beyond the small amount of labor necessary to prepare such things for the table. Household furniture was all made by hand out of rough timber and with crude tools. An ax, a saw and a drawing knife and a few plain augers and chisels of different sizes constituted the full kit of tools of the best equipped workmen. With such tools were made all the chairs, stools, benches, tables and bedsteads. There was not a bureau, sideboard, washstand or wardrobe in the whole county. Such a thing as a piece of painted or varnished furniture of any kind was unheard of. There was not even a saw mill anywhere in reach of the pioneer settler. Sixty years ago a furnished room contained a bed, a few rough chairs and stools and a long bench, a dining table and a cupboard made of boxes or rough cheap boards. The average residence had but one room, which served all the purposes of a parlor, sitting room, library, family room, bedroom, kitchen and dining room. A brief description of a fashionable bedstead will give the reader an idea as to the general character of household furniture, and illustrate how it could all be made from rough lumber by awkward workmen with a few crude tools, already described. A bedstead had but one leg or post, which stood near one corner of the cabin. The distance from the lone post to the log walls of the cabin was about four feet in one direction and seven feet in another. These distances measured the width and length of the bed. The leg or post was simply a stick of timber about as large as a man's leg, and as high as his waist, split from a tree, hewed square with an ax, and smoothly dressed with a drawing knife. Large auger holes were bored in two sides of the post near the top, and similar holes were made in the logs in the walls of the cabin at the same height. Two pieces of timber prepared after the same manner as the post, one four feet long and the other seven, served as rails of the bedstead. The ends of the rails were trimmed to fit the holes in post and walls, and one end of each rail was driven into a hole in the post and the other driven into a hole in the cabin wall. This made the framework of the bedstead. Rough clapboards were placed over this frame after the manner of slats, and dry cow hide, hair turned up, was spread over the clapboards to complete the groundwork of the bed. Economy, utility and durability were the strong points of these old-time bedsteads. The people in that early day had no locks to anything. It is told as a story perhaps, that the first lock that ever came into Hopkins County was bought by a farmer and attached to the door of his corn crib. It aroused the indignation of the whole neighborhood and the people in mass meeting assembled and compelled him to remove it. They held that it was a reflection upon the honesty of the neighborhood, and an insult to the whole community. They freely granted that he had a perfect right to lock things from his own children in his own house if he felt so disposed, but to turn a key in the face of the whole community was a public insult they would not submit to.

CHAPTER VI.

A CHAPTER FULL OF INCIDENTS.

The following interesting matter has been gathered here and there over the country and can be relied upon as historical facts without exaggeration. Robert Hargrave built the first blacksmith shop in the county. It was built at old Sulphur Bluff. He made the first plow, it was called "cary plow" the only plow used at that time. A bar share, a long iron share and a wooden moldboard. When it struck a root or stump or other solid substance, the handles would fly up with a quick jerk and drop back with a vigorous punch. When it came to a root, it gave you no warning at all, but slowly sneaked under the thing so far that you had to back your team to get it out. If the root was weak and yielding enough it would break and both ends of the broken root would come at your defenseless shins with force sufficient to skin them from ankles to knees. This old time plow tested the piety of the old time settler. Corn was plowed five times and about five furrows to the row. A very small amount of cotton was raised in Hopkins County in an early day. The people did a great deal of unnecessary work and in the very hardest way possible. Wheat was raised to a limited extent and cut with a cradle, and then threshed with flails. The way of making flails was simply to cut a hickory sapling long enough for both the handle and the club. At the place where the handle was to end and the club to begin, they beat a section of the sapling a few inches long, with the back of an axe, till it was a mere withe and perfectly flexible. They laid the wheat on the floor of the barn or on a covered pen of rails and pounded it to a mass of chaff, broken straw and wheat. This work was always done in the hottest days of summer. When the wheat was threshed, they sifted through a riddle made for the purpose to separate the wheat from the straw and coarse particles of chaff. In sifting the wheat, all the finer chaff that was small enough to go through the holes in the home made sieve or riddle would remain in the wheat. To separate it from the wheat one man would pour wheat and chaff together, in a small stream, from a vessel held high above his head, while two other men fanned vigorously, with a sheet or bed quilt, as it fell. Within a few years the flail was dispensed with and oxen were used to tramp the wheat. Horses or oxen walked around in a circle upon the wheat, till the wheat straw was thoroughly tramped to pieces and wheat completely threshed. The wheat was then cleaned in a manner as above described. Times have changed since then sure enough. There were no large slave holders in Hopkins County. There were a great many who owned a few slaves they were always fed and clothed well. A few of the old time negroes are here now. They were the happiest people on earth, never had the blues or gave way to despondency. All the world was indeed a stage to them and life was but a comic farce. The old time slave negro has no patience with the partially educated "smart Elick" negro of to-day. The simple customs of these old pioneers began gradually to pass away with the introduction of modern machinery which has wrought a great revolution in our county, but its introduction has not decreased the expense of living. Gallantry among the old pioneers was a leading characteristic, there were no women in the eyes of such men, all females of human kind were ladies. Hospitality was another leading trait in the old timer. The traveler found a hearty welcome in every home, and the wealth of the host was always lavished upon the traveler with a delicacy of taste and sincerity of hospitality such as would insure his comfort and enjoyment. No remuneration was expected, or would be accepted, for such hospitality. The whole social atmosphere was redolent with this generous spirit.

J. P. (Uncle Perry) Hargrave, who has linked his name permanently with the history of Hopkins County, was born in the state of Indiana in the year of 1821. He moved to Texas in the section in which he now lives in the year of 1842 with his father William Hargrave and his brother Harvey. J. P. Hargrave married Casanda Clark, a lady who had lived in Texas since the year of 1834 in Red River County, in 1848. They have raised only two chil-

dren, John C. and Charles J. They are both good
and useful citizens, and live near their aged parents.
When Mr. Hargrave came into the territory there
was only one family living in what is now Hopkins
County, a Mr. Bivens, who soon disappeared and
nothing was ever heard of him or his family. It
was supposed that they were all massacred by the
wild tribes of Indians. The territory soon began
to be settled by good but adventurous citizens. The
last election of the Republic of Texas was held at
old Sulphur Bluff. Ned Burleson and Ausen Jones
were the candidates. Ausen Jones was the successful candidate. During this time other settlers
came into the territory. Billy Barker, Robert E.
Mansell and Billy Mathis. Johnson Wren located
in the northwestern part of the county and was the
first representative in the State Legislature. Capt.
M. Brannon came into the district about this time.
Nash Cole was the first to locate at Black Jack
Grove. The Jordan family moved in about the same
time. The county was created in the year 1845, and
organized in 1846. Unfortunately there appears
to be some misunderstanding in reference to the
name given the county. Some of the old timers
claim that the county was named in honor of Eldridge Hopkins, while J. P. Hargrave declares that
the county was named in honor of the Hopkins
family. When the county had been surveyed,
which was done by Robert Hargraves, the Legislature of Texas appointed a committee, consisting
of Robert Hargrave, Capt. Eli Hopkins, Billy Barker,

James Ward and Billy Wilkins, to locate the center of the county for a county site. They began on the southwest corner of Lamar County and ran a line by mathematical calculation, with their surveying equipage to within a few hundred yards of where the old town of Tarrant once stood, and drove in a post. It was therefore finally decided to locate the county site at Tarrant. The day the county site was located which was accomplished by vote, the county officials were chosen. In the year 1843 the wild Indians made a raid on the Birdwell neighborhood, on the south side of North Sulphur creek. Upon information of the Indians being in the county, the male portion of every family in the county left their homes and went in search of the enemy. They simply passed through without doing any serious damage save stealing a horse now and then. On the return from the Indian hunt the men came upon a large black bear near where the ladies, wives and daughters of the gentlemen, were corralled in one small log cabin. When they fired upon the bear, the ladies stampeded and were frightened almost out of their wits.

The first hewed log house was built by Glen Hargrave, all the neighbors were invited to aid in erecting this building. On this occasion Eldridge Hopkins came in too late to put in a day's work. They all combined to court martial Mr. Hopkins, he replied, "I have a good excuse." He was asked to give it at once; he went to his horse and brought up three panther skins; he had shot and killed three panthers on his trip that morning. He was excused of course. In the winter of 1845, in riding from Joe Leright's place on Clarksville road to where J. C. Brewer now lives, a distance of eight miles, Uncle Perry Hargrave counted one hundred and sixty deer. The same year he stood upon the spot where Harmon Gregg now lives, and counted fifty deer at a sight. Wild horses were to be seen often in droves. They were called mustangs, and were worthless and troublesome. The bear, which were black, lay in the brush, never coming out, except to pass from one point to another. They were the hog's greatest enemy. Wolves were very numerous and annoyed the settlers by howling in large groups and in many other ways. The panther was dreaded perhaps more than any other animal of the forest. They were viscious and very destructive to everything within their power. They would, with the silent tread of a cat, steal upon their prey and destroy it with great ferociousness.

The first marriage that took place in Hopkins County was consummated in October, 1843. The contracting parties were Thos. C. Clark and Elizabeth B. Hargrave. The marriage ceremony was performed by Abner McKinzie, justice of the peace of Clarksville. The first death in the territory was W. W. Hargrave, he was buried at the McFall burying ground. He was the first person buried in this now famous grave yard. Uncle Perry was the first person in the county to arrive at his majority. He attended the first camp meeting, which was held in the brush, and was a great success. Rev. Joe Bishop was the first man to preach in the county. He was a primitive Baptist and could not read print, but his text could always be found "twixt" lids of the Bible, somewhere "twixt" Generations and Revolutions. He was honest and sincere and faithful in the discharge of his duty.

CHAPTER VII.

Sam W. Smith was born in Mason County, Kentucky, on the 17th day of March, 1824. In the year of 1846 he moved with his father, Gilbert Smith, to Hopkins County, Texas, where he remained for a short time, and returned to his native state where he had been engaged in steamboating. While absent from Texas he met Miss Mary Johnson, an Ohioan by birth, with whom he became engaged. Subsequently he returned to Texas and married Miss Minerva Hopkins, daughter of Eldridge Hopkins. By this union eleven children were born to them. There are at this time nine of these children living, Wm. J., Sam G., Mary J., Harvey G., Mary E., Patrick H., Richard R., Callin C., and David R. They are all good and useful citizens and tax payers of the county. In the year of 1853 Sam W. Smith was elected sheriff of Hopkins County. Mr. Smith served his people with such satisfaction that they retained him in office as sheriff for twelve years. He had the misfortune to lose his wife in the year of 1874. Within a few years he learned from information that Miss Johnson was a widow, she having married also, and lived in Emporia, Kansas. In the year of

1876 he visited Emporia and met Mrs. Mary Orbison, and they were made man and wife. During a trip up Red River with his boat, just after his engagement with Miss Johnson, when he had gone up as far as Fulton the water had fallen to such a low ebb that he, crew, boat and all were detained all summer. This was in the spring and they were to be married in June. By mutual agreement the marriage was postponed indefinitely.

When Mr. Smith was elected sheriff there were only five hundred voters in Hopkins County. This was in 1853. Of the citizens who voted in 1849 there are living to-day in the county, Sam W. Smith, Lodwick Vaden, Dave Hopkins, Perry Hargrave, Henry Barclay, Henry Russell and Frank Pierce.

The first man that was killed in the county after its organization was William Harper, an uncle of Strong Harper. He was killed by Jessie C. Russell. This act was committed in the court house at old Tarrant. The second man that was killed was Richard Crook, the first county clerk in the county. He was killed by Bushrod Musgrove near White Oak creek. This creek was dry except in a few places which the water had washed into holes. Mr. Crook had enclosed one of these holes of water for the use, benefit and convenience of the people in the immediate neighborhood. Bushrod Musgrove had cattle under herd. He drove this herd of cattle to the hole of water that Mr. Crook had enclosed. Crook was at the hole of water when Musgrove came with his herd of cattle. The difficulty occurred at this hole of water where Crook was killed. The few people in the county were indignant. It spread consternation over the whole county. Farmers left their plows in the middle of the field and all business stopped as suddenly as if the angel of doom had sounded the knell of time. Musgrove escaped punishment, but was afterwards killed at Jefferson. His body was sewed up in a sack and cast into Cypress Bayou, where it was found by some fishermen. The third killing in Hopkins County was that in which Armstead Payne was killed by Wash. Thomas. Soon after Thomas killed Payne he killed John Hill, and soon after this killing of Payne and Hill, Thomas was killed by one Vansion, a sheep raiser. Vansion was not punished by the laws of his county for the commission of this act, but was left to the God of Heaven to determine the justice or injustice of the deed. The thought is simply horrifying, to appear before the judgment bar of God with our hands stained with the blood of our kind, and strange to say these three men were killed within one quarter of a mile of each other.

Sam W. Smith was young when these terrible and exciting incidents transpired. He is an old man now, but his memory is exceptionally good, he has a bright and vigorous mind and remembers every county official from the organization of the county to the present time. The district judges were John T. Mills, Wm. S. Todd, Byrd Gray, H. P. Mabry, Green J. Clark, J. A. B. Putmen, E. W. Terhoone, H. C. Connor. The sheriffs were Bartholomew Millhollan, H. C. Russell, Jesse Russell, A. B. Hudson, Sam W. Smith, who served twelve years, J. A. Weaver served eight years, John R. Furgeson six years. Sam G. Smith, William Branon, Bascom Sherman served six years, George Withers four years, Wilbur Loving is serving his second term. The county judges were D. O. Horton, John P. Reeves, Elias Wallis, William Houghton, A. G. Melton, L. G. Harmon, G. H. Crowder, F. M. Rogers, J. M. Morris, H. C. Connor, R. B. Keasler, who is serving his third term. The county clerks were Richard Crook, Eldridge Hopkins, R. E. Mathews, Z. C. Mathews, Ambrose Edwards, A. P. Landers, Jas. W. Avera, John Cox, J. C. Avera, present clerk. The district clerks were J. Bottoms, Dr. R. H. Scott, Wm. M. Ewing, E. F. Scott, J. M. Ashcroft, J. W. Avera, Jasper Thomas, W. J. Cline, Asa Ramsey, John Furgerson, present clerk. The names of the county attorneys, the assessors and collectors, have not been given in or they certainly would have appeared in this important list of county officials. In after years reference to this list will furnish important and useful information to the reader of the history of Hopkins County. Sam W. Smith is the oldest living sheriff in the Lone Star State.

BIOGRAPHIES.

BIOGRAPHY OF DAVE HOPKINS.

This grand old Texas hero was born in the state of Indiana in the year 1825. He is therefore seventy-seven years of age. He came to Texas with his parents when he was only fifteen years old. He has lived in the state for sixty-two years. His parents died in Red River County and are buried at the old McKinzie burial ground. He came into what is now Hopkins County in the year 1844. It was at that time a republic, and very few people had ventured to cross over the trackless swamps of the Sulphur creeks. These creek bottoms were considered a howling wilderness and dangerous and impracticable for the travelers to undertake to pass through without an informed guide.

Dave Hopkins married Miss Annie Hargrave, daughter of James Hargrave, in the year 1846. There was no authority in the county to grant permit to marry, therefore he was compelled to go to Paris for license to wed Miss Hargrave. He married his wife in the neighborhood of where he has lived all of his life. There were seven children born to them, four of this number are living, Josh E. married Miss Sudie Gregg, Susan married Joe. W. Connor, Ellen married James Donagee, he died and she afterwards married

A. P. Hudson, Sallie married William Smith, son of Dr. Smith, an old pioneer citizen, John Howard married Miss Emmie Staten, a young lady of good birth and excellent family. When Mr. Hopkins (Uncle Dave) came into Hopkins County, it was known as Red River District, and very few people were living anywhere near him. He refers with pride to Rev. Joe Bishop, whose name has been previously mentioned in connection with this history.

As the only authorized agent anywhere in the whole county to perform the marriage ceremony, Rev. Bishop was a primitive Baptist preacher and could not read print. The Hardshell Baptist as they were called were the dominant religious party in the country. In fact they had almost a monopoly of religion among the people. They would never accept any remuneration at all and to the very last they protested and argued against the principle. of paying preachers anything for their services. A little later the voice of the ubiquitous Methodist circuit rider was heard in the land, and in his wake came the Cumberland Presbyterian preachers and evangelists. Their coming inaugurated a war of words touching man's free agency and God's predestination, and stirred up no little bitterness and strife among the settlers. Preachers began to wear their coats while they were preaching, and to give the chapter and verse where the text could be found. There were no Sunday Schools, but singing schools flourished in every neighborhood. The schools were in different neighborhoods, and as the country was sparsely settled and neighborhoods were few and far between, a singing teacher would often ride on horseback sixty or seventy-five miles a week to complete the circuit and visit all his schools. The preachers of that day would give blood-curdling descriptions of the lake which burns with fire and brimstone. Their descriptions of hell and the intense agony of the damned were perfectly appalling. The preachers firmly believed it all, and the people never for a moment doubted it. Rev. Joe Bishop had a brother whose name was Oliver, a mechanic of great importance to the settlers. He manufactured all the chairs for the people for miles around. Uncle Dave has one of these chairs in his house at this time of his make, a curious and strange piece of architecture and wonderful piece of furniture in this day and generation. This old chair is now worn and in a dilapidated condition, but it serves to demonstrate the fact that the pioneer settler was not without invention and ingenuity. He had this chair made expressly for his wife at the birth of her second child, Susan. He takes pleasure in referring to Robert Hargrave as being one of the most useful men to his county in that day. Robert Hargrave was the founder of the old and new Sulphur Bluff. He built the first mill and the first gin that was built in Hopkins County. He was strictly sober, and religiously opposed to the sale of liquor, therefore no whisky

was ever sold in Sulphur Bluff as long as he had
control of affairs there. The morals of the village
have been exceptionally good,—never a man killed
in the place.

At the time Dave Hopkins came into the district there was living in the neighborhood an old
time doctor. His name was South. Dr. South
did all the doctoring for the settlers for miles around,
being the only doctor in all the county. He was
entirely illiterate, could not read a line in any
book, but strange to say, he was eminently successful, seldom losing a patient, and in cases of obstetrics
he was a great success. His efforts as a doctor
were attended with most wonderful results, and
he was considered a remarkable physician by all
the old pioneers, who had him called in on all occasions of distressing sickness. He dressed in a
manner so odd as to often excite remarks, and on
one occasion when he was referred to as being a
splendid physician, a stranger being present and
observing the unique style of dress said: "If I
had been called upon to shoot a doctor I would
never have pointed my gun towards that man.
His charges were liberal and satisfactory to his
customers. Mr. Hopkins is living on his father's
head-right, he began building the house in which
he now lives in the year 1860. The house is old
now and shows signs of decay, as does its owner.
Old Time with its devastating hand has made
its impression on all the surroundings. There
stand in his yard a few old scarred and storm-

shaken seedling pear trees that were planted by the hand of the woman he led to the altar when she was a sweet, blushing maiden, and who lived for years to help him bear the burdens, the trials, hardships, afflictions and disappointments of life. She has passed away to wait in heaven with the angels for the coming of her companion. She has sat in the evenings under the shade of these old pear trees and sung sweet lullabies to her children and waited with feelings of love and affection for the approach of her husband from his daily toil. Mr. Hopkins is a Prohibitionist and a devout member of the Methodist church, liberal in his views, conservative in his ideas, and consistent in his actions. He is seventy-seven years old, in good health, and promises to live for a while yet. He is a brother to Joslin and Harry Hopkins, both deceased, an uncle to Frank Hopkins of Sulphur Springs, who is loved for his sobriety, honesty and general manhood.

BIOGRAPHY OF HENRY BARCLAY.

This old Mexican warrior is familiarly known all over the county as Uncle Henry. He moved to Texas with his father, Hugh Barclay, in the year 1845. The United States and the Republic of Mexico were engaged in a war. In the year 1846 young Barclay volunteered and went to Mexico to fight the Mexicans, under Gen. Zachary Taylor. He was engaged in the battle of Monterey and had the satisfaction of seeing the Mexican General, Ampudia, surrender himself and his army to the American General. He then returned to Texas, where he had left his father, and the entire family moved at once to Hopkins County. This was during the fall of 1846. Hopkins County had just been organized and the county site selected.

Mr. Barclay was a farmer and a number one blacksmith, and rendered great service as a smith to the new settlers of the county. Blacksmiths were in great demand. Material to work with was in greater demand. Uncle Henry has made many weeding hoes, in fact he manufactured everything that was wanted when material could be found or obtained in any manner to be used for such purposes. In the year 1853 he married Miss Sarilda Hargrave, sister to Perry Hargrave. One child was born to them, a girl. She is dead now. He lost his wife within less than one year after marriage. Subsequently he married Mrs. Brant. Three children were born to this union, only one of whom—Margaret—is living at this time. She is the wife of Charles Kiker, a plain, unassuming gentleman with industrious habits. They live at the home of Mrs. Kiker's father, and cared for and looked to his comfort and wants in his declining years. Uncle Henry is living upon the same tract of land he settled fifty years ago. He is living in a log house that was built by Enoch Chapman fifty-two years ago. Many of the old settlers will remember the sad and deplorable death of Mr. Chapman. Tired of life he sought relief in death by his own hand. This house has been in constant use for fifty-two years, The logs are post oak, and are apparently as sound to-day as when first placed in the walls of the house. The cracks are chinked and daubed in the old-fashioned way which has been fully described heretofore in this history. The old-time chimney extending almost entirely across one end of the house, indeed quite old in this day of progress, style and fashion. Mr. Barclay's home is situated on the brow of a red clay hill overlooking the Sulphur creek bottom lands, which has ever been dense and thickly set with forest growth, vines, cane and briars. This bottom was a great rendezvous for wild beasts and animals of all description. He has stood in his yard in an early day and killed deer, and has been annoyed with panthers, bears, catamounts, wolves, wild cats, and the gray eagle, all of which he has killed in his day. There are many people living in Hopkins County now, who are no strangers to the effect which the howling of wolves in a dense forest at night will produce upon the whole nervous system of a lonely belated traveler, or upon some lonely woman waiting late at night for the return of her husband. The whole county was then, compared with its present condition, uninhabited and unbroken forest, infested with wolves, panthers, bears, deer and other wild animals. The people had no method of travel but walking or riding on horseback or in ox carts.

There was absolutely no medium by which ideas of any kind could be communicated from one settlement to another except in the head of a horseman or footman. The inhabitants of any section rarely ever saw or heard about anything which took place beyond the limits of their neighborhood. The styles and fashions of every community therefore had at least the merit of originality. Hogs were very scarce in Mr. Barclay's neighborhood. On one occasion he took his ox cart and went away down the country below where Mt. Pleasant is now located and bought a sow and pigs. The mast was bountiful, acorns, nuts, and a multiplicity of wild grapes, called the mustang grape, grew in profusion all over the wild woods. When he returned to his home with his hogs, he made pens and put the pigs into the pen and turned the sow loose upon the range. Mr. Barclay had noticed bear signs around his premises, and knowing it was the nature of the hog to dread the bear above all other beasts, was uneasy. The sow came regularly to her pigs for a few evenings, and then disappeared as suddenly as if the ground had opened and swallowed her. He learned afterward that the sow had gone back to where he had got her from, a distance of forty miles. She had seen a bear, took fright and left her pigs. The hog looks upon the bear as its mortal enemy.

Mr. Barclay has been a member of The Christian Church for a great number of years. He has lived a consistent life. He is loved for his liberal spirit and generous qualities, and is fond of company, and appreciates a visit from his neighbors and friends, and takes much pleasure in talking over old times. He is burdened with the weight of eighty-three years and not in the enjoyment of good health.

BIOGRAPHY OF JAMES D. CLIFTON.

INDIAN TROUBLES.

James D. Clifton, an old pioneer citizen, a plain, unassuming farmer, came with his parents into the state of-Texas in the year 1837. He was a boy at that time eight years of age. He lived in Titus County for a while and afterward came over into Hopkins County. When he came across Red River all the country lying south of Cypress Bayou was known as Nacogdoches District. Texas was at this time a republic, and the country wild and rough. At the age of twenty-seven years he met Miss Eliza Hudson of Hopkins County, with whom he fell deeply in love. They afterwards married. Four children have been born to them. They are all living in Hopkins County, Miss Mattie married Monroe Dawson, a gentleman of splendid ancestry and one that no lady would be ashamed to bear his name, a prominent merchant and an all round business man. J. H. married Miss Mattie Gregg, Turner married Miss Kate McCoy, daughter of a worthy old pioneer citizen. David is yet single and lives with his aged parents and has control of his father's plantation and his business affairs.

Mr. Clifton has been a great hunter, and has killed every kind of animal and beast that was common to this country, except a mustang horse. He has killed buffalo, panther, catamount, bear, wild cat, deer, otters, rattlesnakes and pole cats. It would require page after page to give an account of the wild, hazardous, hair-breadth escapes he has experienced in these hunts, but the reader must know, if only from imagination, that buffalo, bear and panther hunting is both exciting and dangerous. The hides or skins of these animals are all profitable and considered quite valuable. There has been a demand in the eastern and northern markets for the skin of such animals, and when it was possible for the people in that day to market these skins, they brought to them considerable revenue. Mr. Clifton relates an interesting but a sad and grievous incident of the massacre of the Ripley family about seven miles below where Mount Vernon in Franklin County is now located. Mr. Ripley had moved from the Old States and settled with his family on this place. He had erected a small log cabin almost insufficient to afford comfort for his large family, which consisted of ten in number. On this occasion he had business of importance to look after in Red River County and was absent from his home and family when this deplorable affair occurred. About two o'clock in the afternoon his two oldest daughters were in the cabin and heard an unusual noise, the crack of a gun which fell upon their ears like

the crack of doom. They both with one accord
sprang to the opening in the cabin. To their
horror and distress they saw a band of wild Indians
advancing at a rapid pace toward their cabin.
With a maniacal scream they jumped from the
opening in the cabin, and with lightning speed,
horrified and distressed, hid themselves in the
dense wild woods near by. The Indians, with a
demoniacal war whoop, rushed upon the cabin in
the woods and massacred every one of the family,
eight in number. The mother, who was sick in
bed with an infant child, fourteen days old, was
instantly killed by the savages. A sister, who had
taken the child from its mother's breast an
attempted to shield and protect the little infant,
was killed and the child was taken by the Indians
and its head was thrown against a tree just outside
of the yard and its brains were scattered in all
directions. This tree was standing a few years
ago when Mr. Clifton last saw it. Henry Stout
and John Denton the following spring gathered
a small company of men, getting some from the
state of Arkansas, and followed the Indian trail.
They came upon the Indians about half-way between Dallas and where Fort Worth is located at
present. They had a small village. The men
burnt the village and shot and killed a few of the
Indians. While the village was on fire they pursued the Indians. The Indians ambushed the
company of white men and killed John Denton
and wounded Henry Stout. Henry Stout is the

father of that grand old patriot, champion bear hunter and trailer of thieves, Sealin Stout. John Cullom was engaged in this Indian fight. John Cullom is now dead. He was an old pioneer of Hopkins County. The two Ripley girls who had such a close call, who so narrowly escaped assassination by this mob of murderous Indians, were hunted up the next day, and when found they were demented, having partially lost their reason during the time that had intervened between the massacre of the family and their departure from the cabin in the woods. During the long black night that they wandered in the lonely thicket, they had become separated, and were alone when found. They well remembered the wild shrieks and screams, the prayers and appeals for mercy, that filled the atmosphere of the entire woods for many feet around. They well knew that these frantic screams and cries for mercy came from those whom they loved so much, and that they had, perhaps every one, been slaughtered by those brutal and cruel savages. One of the girls was discovered the next morning about nine o'clock, the other was not found till late the following evening. Denton Creek, that divides Denton County from other counties, was named in honor of John Denton, who fell a victim to the Indians while defending with his life this unfortunate family. A monument should be erected over his grave by the state of Texas, and his last resting place should be marked with honors to his memory for his gallantry and bravery on that occasion. Away back in an early day a man and his family had come to Texas and were traveling in a wagon, and he was cutting his road as he went. He used a compass as a guide. Somewhere, not far from where Mount Pleasant is now located, they camped for the night, spread their buffalo rugs and retired. Indians attacked them during the night and shot nine arrows into the body of the man, and—strange to relate—he was the only member of the family that was injured by the Indians. Mr. Clifton's father had this wounded man taken to his house, the arrows extracted and medical aid given him. He recovered, though it required about twelve months time for him to recover. Mr. Clifton is esteemed as an upright and conscientious man, and possesses the respect and warm regards of a wide circle of acquaintances. He has been a useful citizen in the county. Now, when he looks back over his past life he has nothing to regret.

BIOGRAPHY OF GLEN HARGRAVE.

REMINISCENCES.

E. G. Hargrave is a son of Harvey Hargrave, whose name has been mentioned in this history. He was born in the state of Indiana in the year 1839. He came to Texas with his father in the year 1842. He was, therefore, only three years old at the time. He has been raised in Hopkins County and has lived continuously in the county since 1845. He married Miss M. E. Chapman, daughter of Benjamin Chapman, in the year 1857. This union is a happy one. They have had ten children born to them. Eight of these children are living. Isaac A. married Miss Eliza Coleman, she died and he afterwards married Miss Laura Oxford. John W. lives at Coke in Wood County, and is a practicticing physician. Mary E. married Joe Coleman, now living in Haskell County. Robert L. is also a physician, he married Miss Mae Adams. Joseph W. married Miss Belle Healy and lives near his parents. Thomas M. married Miss Ruth Helm and lives on his father's plantation. Miss Dona C. is yet single, so is Miss Della. They are both nice, sweet young ladies and are a credit to their parents and an honor to Hopkins County. Mr. Hargrave has engaged in agricultural pursuits and has always had plenty of this world's goods to make him and those dependent upon him comfortable and happy. He has reared an industrious and useful family, and he and his companion have much to be thankful for in this regard. He has been a lifelong Democrat and has no patience with any kind of "isms." There is no family in Hopkins County that enjoys the confidence of the people to a greater degree than does this family. His inhabitiveness is great, having lived all of his married life upon one tract of land. He has never had any public career, having no taste for that kind of life, preferring instead to pursue the even tenor of his way as a common citizen, satisfied with the faithful discharge of his duties as such to his country, to his friends, his neighbors and his God. Being reared in Texas he is not a stranger to the hardships incumbent upon the early settler, and has experienced all of these things in common with other pioneers of Hopkins County. He relates an incident of facts worthy of mention and which will be read with deep interest. In the year 1846 his father was out from home looking for bee trees, which were quite common then, watching the holes of water where the bees were satisfying their thirst. He soon observed the direction in which the bees were flying, and immediately followed the course the bees were taking. In a large, unbroken cane brake not far distant stood a couple of massive oak trees. He climbed up a sapling near by in order to enable himself to look over the tops of the tall cane to look into one of the large trees for bees. In sighting up and down the tree (it requires one with great perception to find a bee tree) his attention was attracted to a cub bear lying at the root of one of the huge trees hard by. He retraced his steps to his house and returned with his hired hand to assist in catching the young bear. Mr. Hargrave could have accomplished this feat alone had he not been molested by the mother of the cub. The cane in the thicket was so dense and so thick that ingress to the cub was impossible. They were armed with large hack knives which were used vigorously. There was a deep ditch some twelve feet wide that impeded their approach to the young bear. The cane was cut as a means of escape when the cub was captured. When everything was clear, Harvey Hargrave said to Brandon, his hired hand: "You take the gun, and in case the old bear attempts to fight when I capture the cub, you shoot her; or you go after the cub and I will stand sentinel." Brandon preferred to stand guard. Mr. Hargrave advanced slowly and cautiously and captured the cub, which began to cry and squall at the top of its voice. Mr. Hargrave choked the cub and ran for dear life in the direction of his sentinel, who, when he heard the cub squall, became nervous and his legs carried his body off in spite of his heart's desire to remain and see his friend out. When Mr. Hargrave came to where he had left him with the gun, he looked ahead and saw Brandon running at a rapid gait with gun in hand some sixty yards off. This flight of Brandon came near causing Mr. Hargrave choking the young bear to death. It, however, revived and was tamed for a pet. On the following Sunday Mr. Hargrave summoned all of his neighbors, who were few in number, to assemble at his house for the purpose of securing the old bear and capturing the remaining cubs. There were two cub bears left at the big tree. The crowd of neighbors soon gathered in and immediately hastened to the place where they anticipated an exciting and interesting time. They all knew that the bears were housed in the hollow of this big old tree. Some had axes, others guns, and all had trusty dogs. It was unanimously agreed that the big tree should be felled to the earth, at which time they all expected to have a great frolic with dogs and bear. In bright anticipation of this expected fun, they began cutting upon the tree. The noise of the crowd of men and great number of dogs together with the strokes upon the tree with the axes brought the old bear from her hiding place. She immediately started to the ground, tail foremost. It is the custom of this animal to go up head foremost and return tail foremost. As she approached the ground she was shot several times but not very seriously. A boy with a small rifle then shot and killed the bear, having made a fortunate shot by striking over the region of the heart. This boy's name was Jacob Brant, who subsequently became the father of Willis Brant, a well-known and respected citizen of Hopkins County. Mr. Hargrave gave one of the cubs to Jacob Brant, who domesticated it, and finally exchanged it with David Clark for a ewe sheep. This transaction occurred in the year 1846. Young Brant retained this ewe and her increase until the year 1861, when he had accumulated a large flock of sheep, amounting to over three hundred head. This bit of historical information is worthy of emulation by all young men who are starting out in life. E. G. Hargrave is sixty-three years of age, has lived in Texas sixty years and is, in common parlance, a thoroughbred Texan.

BIOGRAPHY OF REV. JOE HOOTEN.

Joseph Hooten was born in the State of Tennessee, in the year 1824. He came to Hopkins County in the year 1848 and located in the same section where he has lived all of his long and useful life. He married Miss Manda Strother soon after he came into the county. By this union ten children were born to them, six of these are living. They all live near their parents, their eldest and youngest live at home with their aged parents and are a comfort and a joy to them in the evening of their days. Mr. Hooten is known all over the county as Uncle Joe. He has been a minister of the Gospel for 52 years. He is noted for his veracity, integrity, and honesty, and his children will inherit an untarnished escutcheon, a legacy more valuable than gold. He is of the Christian faith and has taken great numbers of people into his church through baptism. His ministry has been eminently successful. Since he has been preaching the gospel he has united in the holy bonds of matrimony 520 couples, and out of this vast multiplicity of marriages only four of these couples have disagreed to a point of separation. He has been useful to his country in many ways; has acted in the capacity of school teacher ever since he came into the county. He has taught the fathers to read, their sons to read, unto the third generation, and it is said to his credit as an honest sincere Christian gentleman that no man who was taught by him for the length of five months' time was ever sent to the penitentiary for the commission of crime.

The great mass of his students have made Christians and useful citizens in the community in which they are living. He has lived the life of personal purity, and is absolutely incorruptable and feels that when he is called to his long rest in the shades that eternal happiness awaits him. His companions till lives to brighten his home. He, with this noble woman, who has been his solace and his comfort in hours of trouble, and who hand in hand together have ascended the hill of life, now look back over the path they traveled, seeing the hardships they have endured, remembering, too, the pleasures they have enjoyed, no doubt their hearts fill with gratitude when they can say we have nothing to fear in the great beyond, we will soon pass to our reward.

BIOGRAPHY OF J. J. MARTIN.

J. J. Martin was born in Alabama and reared in the State of Tennessee. He is an octogenarian and has lived in Texas since 1845. He came to Hopkins County 45 years ago. He married Miss Nancy Everett in Cass County, Texas, at the age of 29 years. By this union six children were born. She passed away at the birth of her last child. J. B. and C. D. Martin and Mrs. James Lee are all children of this union. They are all well known citizens of Hopkins County, honest, upright in their dealings. He next married Miss Elvy Gardner, of Hopkins County. There is no issue living from this marriage. This wife died and he afterwards married Mrs.

Pickel, four children were born to this marriage. Two are living, one is living with his aged parents and looks after his father's business affairs. This wife passed away and he then married Mrs. Penington, who still lives. Mr. Martin has followed agricultural pursuits all of his life and is a successful farmer and taxpayer in the county. He is an old Confederate soldier. He has been a member in good standing in the Methodist church for 61 years and expects to die in the faith. He has never been in public life, having no taste in that direction. He is most highly esteemed for his earnest upright Christian character. He is a man of kind disposition, is affable, genial and hospitable, and makes friends wherever he goes. He is 80 years old.

BIOGRAPHY OF LODWICK VADEN.

Lodwick (Uncle Lodwick) Vaden was born in Smith County, Tennessee, on January 29, 1817. At this time he is 85 years of age, a hale, hearty old gentleman of wonderful vitality. He married Miss Nancy E. Dowdle when he was 23 years old, in the State of Mississippi. By this union ten children came to them, whose names are as follows: Miss Mary, married Alonzo De Spain, and are located in DeLeon, Comanche County; Woodson, married Miss Martin; Miss Sallie, married Piney Welch, a prominent well to do citizen of Hopkins County. Miss Judie is yet single and resides with her aged parents, to whom she is devoted. She is a bright, interesting lady, and has by her kindly disposition and noble qualities of heart, gathered around her aged parents' home many encouraging and admiring friends.   Miss Fannie, married Thos. Wood, a kindly disposed and worthy gentleman, a farmer and tax-payer of the county.   Mr. Vaden emigrated to Hopkins County in the year 1845, just one year before the county was organized.   He has been a citizen of Hopkins County for 57 years.   There were only a few people living in the county when he came to it.   The families who were here were the Hargraves, Hopkins, Brandon, Wren, Barker, Abb Neatherly, Lindleys, Millhollands, Burckhams and a few others whom he cannot recall.   They were not a sufficient number to organize the county at that time.   Mr. Vaden was at that time a young man full of bright hopes for the future.   That future has passed and now he is quite an aged gentleman. He has followed farming and stock raising all of his life.   His upright character and his manly qualities have endeared him to a wide circle of friends, he has weilded a wide influence for good.   He has ever been highly respected and very popular among all who know him.   He has lived to a good old age and can lay down the burdens of life in the county of his adoption amid the primitive scenes that marked its early settlement.   Abb Neatherly has just died.

When Mr. Vaden came into the territory it was an almost tractless wilderness.   The settlers lived from off the wild game that was to be found everywhere in the country.   They had no mail facilities nearer

than 30 miles distant, there were no schools, and
what preaching was heard, was done in the small
cabins of the pioneer settlers. Water was used
from the creeks and lakes and the family supply
was hauled upon slides and ox carts in kegs and barrels. Shreveport, Louisiana, and Jefferson, Texas,
were the markets for supplies. Oxen were used in
freighting to and from these points. It usually required three and four weeks time to complete one of
these trips. Six and seven yoke of oxen were
hitched by means of a yoke and log chains to a
freight wagon and were driven and managed altogether by a long whip lash and by a motion of the
whip stock. The driver of one of these long trains
of oxen would talk to his team, having each ox in
his team named, it was strange how readily they
became educated to his training. "Woh come broad"
meant in plowing, haw. "Gee back" meant the
reverse. To stop, the driver would place himself
on the left side of his tongue yoke of oxen, for which
was always selected the largest oxen in the team,
throw up his whip stock and lean his body back and
repeat the words "woh-w-o-h w-o-h-e." This was
called in an early day, "speaking in the United
States language to ox teams." These ox teams
were never fed, but were necked together by means
of a short grass rope and the left hand ox hobbled,
this process of necking and hobbling was proceeded
with until the entire team was necked and hobbled.
A few large bells were tied around their necks and
then they were turned loose upon the range to root

for their living which they always got in that day, as the grass grew luxuriantly all over the country. On one occasion Mr. Vaden was out hunting for game with his flint and steel gun, it was on a damp day, his dogs had found a large black bear and had trailed him near to Mr. Vaden in a dense thicket. He attempted to shoot the bear, but the powder in his priming pan had become damp and his gun failed to shoot. He was very much alarmed and left the place hurriedly and was not disturbed, only mentally. There is an unseen hand that guides and protects the good. It has been Mr. Vaden's custom for several years to cut out the timber of one acre of ground and prepare the land for the plow, he is still able to do this work. Recently he rode on horseback to his county seat, Sulphur Springs, a distance of 16 miles, transacted his business and returned in the evening to his quiet home, situated in the timber near the waters of Sulphur creek. He is conversant with the ways of the world and stands ready at all times to make allowances for the faults of others. He is a devout member of the Christian Church and for 65 long years has lived up to its teachings. He has ten great grand-children.

BIOGRAPHY OF WILSHIRE BAILEY.

Mr. Bailey was born in the State of Alabama, in the year 1824, and came to Texas with his parents in the year 1835. He married Miss Gage, a daughter of E. N. Gage, in the year 1852. To this union were

born 8 children, seven of whom are still living, five
girls and two boys. His boys are both married and
are thrifty and well to do farmers and tax payers.
Four of his daughters are married, their husbands
are farmers and stock raisers, are good men, upright
and honest in their business relations, and have the
confidence of the people. Mr. Bailey has led a very
active life, he is a typical Texan, open hearted,
outspoken and impulsive, will fight at the drop of
the hat, is a good clever fellow, knows everybody,
and everybody knows him. He has a good strong
mind, but little education. He likes to be in a
crowd, and can talk against a brass band. He has
one daughter living with him, a nice young lady,
somewhat reserved, yet pleasant and agreeable in
her manners, she is very much devoted to her aged
parents and attached to her country home, a beautiful locations on the prairie, so situated as to have a
lovely view of all the country for miles around.
Mr. Bailey's father stopped when he came to Texas
in the neighborhood of where Clarkesville is now
situated, He remained in camp for about two
years. At this time a war was in progress between
the United States and the Republic of Mexico.
His father was engaged in this war. Upon the
return of his father after peace had been declared,
he moved to a point near Blossom prairie and
settled. His father was a farmer. In a few years
the family moved to Hopkins County, it was Red
River District at that time. Mr. Bailey has been
a resident citizen of the county ever since he came

into the county. With Robinson Crusoe he could say as he stood and viewed the vast wilderness in all of its verdant wilds: "I am master of all I survey." He has seen sights and heard sounds emanating from every living creature common to to Texas clime, some of which sent terror to his heart and caused his hair to stand on end and his cheeks to turn pale as death. The country was a trackless wilderness, No friendly call from human kind—no neighbor's dog to bark—no smoke to rise from the top of an inhabitant's cabin—no mild cow to offer up a friendly and motherly call to her infant calf—nothing to drive away the gloomy monotony of his environment save the sad shrill notes of the whippoorwill, the midnight hooting of the lonely owl, the solemn cooing hen, and the frightful crying of the catamount, and the nightly screams of the panther, and the saddened chanting of the rain crow. To add to these distressing sounds the war whoop of the wild Indians was to be heard in the land. He has lived for months in constant dread of the wild tribes of Indians. He has often been forced to leave his cabin and seek shelter in the brush for safety from the savages. He was a Texas ranger and served his country as such under Captain Mansel Matthews. On one occasion when he was called out by his officer to guard the country against the ravages of the Indians, he and Lieutenant Branom were detailed to ride out a few miles from the camp and look for Indian signs. When about four miles distant from the camp they came suddenly upon a large gang of Indians nestling in the thick brush. There appeared to be about one hundred and fifty in number. They both turned for camp with all possible speed. Mr. Bailey was riding a small mustang pony while Lieutenant Branom was favored with a blooded horse. Bailey's pony ran with lightning speed for a short distance and then began to show signs of fatigue. Lieutenant Branom observed this deplorable condition, and said to Bailey, "Whip up your pony or we will both be captured and killed." Bailey replied: "I am doing all I can." Lieutenant Branom said: "I will ride on into camp and report the situation, but before I go let me ask you to prepare for the worst, and say your prayers." The company at camp, seeing Lieutenant Branom riding with hat in hand and coming toward them with the fury of a tornado, instinctively knew that something awful had transpired with Bailey and Branom. They ran for their horses and arms and proceeded with all possible haste to meet Lieutenant Branom. They all turned after receiving Branom's report and went after the Indians. They met Bailey and all went in pursuit of the Indians. The Indians were overtaken, seven or eight of them killed and only one Ranger wounded. Thus this exciting incident, ludicrous as part of the story appears, ended in driving the enemy of the white man from the country. This occurrence took place in the neighborhood of where Mr. McCombs now lives in Delta County.

Mr. Bailey was happy over the termination of this exciting and alarming incident which left him in possession of his scalp.

BIOGRAPHY OF S. G. COYLE.

S. G. Coyle was born in Osage County, Missouri, in the year 1882, and came to the state of Texas in the year 1846, and lived in the county in the forks of the Sulphur creek, and looked after stock cattle for Dr. O. S. Davis. He had charge of these cattle until he volunteered to go to the Mexican war. While he was attending these cattle for Dr. Davis a party of ruffians, calling themselves Regulators, came suddenly upon him and gave him instructions to leave the country under the penalty of death. His assistants became alarmed at this imperative command and fled. Mr. Coyle felt he had a duty to perform, and he remained, giving his attention to his promised obligation. He at once provided himself with suitable weapons and kept them at all times within his reach. He was never disturbed, only occasionally when the gang of outlaws would ride around his camp, which was situated in a deep forest of wilds. Mr. Coyle volunteered for the term of six months. When his time expired, he, in company with a couple of his comrades, started for Hopkins County across an uninhabited country on poor, worn-out horses. They came upon a few people who were engaged in religious services in a camp. They asked for meat and bread. None was to be had—whereupon Mr. Coyle observing the hide of a beef, asked permission to buy it, remarking: "We will eat the hide, hair and any." At this moment a good, kind-hearted woman stepped forward and raised the lid of a rough box saying: "Come here, my hungry friends, and cut off a piece of this middling meat." Mr. Coyle was jubilant and soon ate to his satisfaction, and he and his comrades left in high glee. Again the following spring he volunteered to go to Mexico to assist General Taylor at the siege of Monterey. Twice Mr. Coyle volunteered to serve his adopted country as a soldier. In the year 1848 he married Ann Hankins, One child was the result of this union. When this child was about one year old its mother died, and Dr. Davis took charge of the motherless child and nursed and cared for it until Mr. Coyle remarried, which he did in the year 1851. This wife was the widow Lindley, and mother of Jim Andy Lindley, who is a well-known citizen of Hopkins County, having reared a large and useful family in the county and lives at this time at Rockdale. Mr. Coyle has lived with this wife forty-seven years. It proved to be a happy marriage. She is dead now. By this marriage six children were born. Three girls and three boys. Only two of this number are living. Mr. Coyle is now a very old man. He is an octogenarian. He is in feeble health; is waiting to be called to go and meet his companions in their eternal home. He has lived the life of a Christian, and his example as an honest, upright and just man has always been good. A good citizen, a happy neighbor, an affectionate husband, and a devoted father. He assisted in the blacksmith shop when Robert Hargrave made the first county seal of Hopkins County. This seal was manufactured at old Sulphur Bluff. This improvised seal was placed upon paper and a blow from a mallet or hammer made the impression and rendered good and efficient services until a better one could be obtained. While Mr. Coyle was a soldier in camp at San Antonio a small band of Indians came into the city with a couple of Spanish girls, whom they had taken captive. They were grown and very beautiful. Col. William Young learned through an interpreter that these Indians had killed the parents of the two young ladies and had another of their sisters in captivity in other quarters, whereupon Col. Young called upon the chief of this band and demanded the release of these girls under the penalty of death in the most tortuous form. The colonel arrested the chief, seated him by a small tree and informed him that unless he sent for and had the sister of these two young ladies brought into his camp at once he should never be allowed to rise from his seat. The next evening she was brought into camp and all three set at liberty and sent to friends.

BIOGRAPHY OF JOSIAH SMITH.

Doctor Josiah Smith, deceased, was born and raised in the state of Georgia. At his majority he married Miss Nannie Morgan and moved to Hopkins County, Texas, in the year 1844 and settled on the spot where he has lived a long and useful life, and finally returned to the state of his nativity and passed into eternity. By this marriage nine children were born to them. Out of this number only two are living—Zylphia, died in infancy; Buford lived to manhood and graduated from McKenzie College, enlisted in the Civil war as a Confederate soldier and died in the army with camp fever. Andrew died with measles at home. David M. Smith, one of the best men the writer ever knew, a man almost without a fault, and absolutely incorruptible. He died at his home in Sulphur Springs, with that awful scourge, cancer of the jaw; married Miss Lu Cade, as pure a woman as ever breathed the breath of life, an affectionate wife, a devoted mother and a sacrificing neighbor. William M. married Sallie Hopkins, daughter of Dave Hopkins. He lost his companion and afterwards married Neely Hay, daughter of Rev. Wm. Hay, she lived only eight months and passed to her long home, subsequently he married Elizabeth McAfee, a daughter of Capt. Wm. Pickens. She was a widow and most excellent lady; they have one child, a son, Welcome, a bright, intelligent lad of nine years of age. Miss Emma married Dr. Robuck and lives in Italy, Ellis County. She is the mother of eleven children, she is dead now, so are eight of her children. Josiah married Miss Lou Rogers and lives in Waxahachie, Ellis County. Miss Sallie lived to be grown and passed away. Miss Susie died at an early age. William lives in the vicinity where he was born and raised, and is a useful citizen in his neighborhood. He has engaged in farming and stocking and has been reasonably successful, although he has suffered many serious losses; added to the calamity of the loss of his two wives. He stands misfortunes, trials and troubles with as much courage and fortitude as is common for manly men to do. He is kind hearted and possessed of a genial disposition, and makes all around him happy. His father was a great philanthropist, and will be remembered with feelings of gratitude by many of the old pioneer citizens of the county.

BIOGRAPHY OF CAPT. MERRETT BRANOM.

Merrett Branom was born in the state of Missouri in the year 1820. At the tender age of nineteen he left his home and came to Texas to seek his fortune, and to make the Lone Star state his future home. Soon after he came upon Texas soil he married Miss Ellen Finley, an old Missouri acquaintance. She was a sister to Ed Finley, who is well known as an honorable, just and esteemed citizen of Hopkins County, and an aunt to our worthy ex-tax-assessor, Dave Finley. By this

marriage thirteen children came to them, six boys
and seven girls. Polly Ann married Wm. Young
a splendid man and a most excellent citizen, W. J.
(Bill) married Miss Nancy Chaffin, he has inherited
the noble traits of his father—a pure, incorruptible
man, has held the office of high sheriff of his county. He is esteemed for his brave, courageous
and manly conduct in all the relations of life,
public and private. Rachale married Dr. Mc-
Farlin, a gentleman of noble birth, and is universally
respected, not only for his professional ability,
but for his amiable disposition and uniform kindness toward all whom he meets. Albert married
Sallie Ward. Harvey married Susan Butler, daughter of Uncle Jim Butler, one of the best men in
the county. Julia Ann married Henry Smith, a
worthy, highly esteemed and much respected
gentleman. They live in Commerce, Hunt County.
Eliza J. married James Ingram. Victoria married
Norman Gillis. Tecuseh married Mattie Welch.
Milton married Beulah Newell. Miss Maloney
Ellen is yet single and lives with her aged mother,
a grand old pioneer woman. Merrett married
Miss Moore. Lucy Branom is also single, she, too,
lives at the home of her maternal parent. Capt.
Merrett Branom is dead. He passed to his long
home to rest in the shade of eternity on January
24th, 1900, to wait the coming of his companion,
who with him bore the burdens, hardships, trials,
disappointments and sorrows of pioneer life. She
is waiting her call with patience and fortitude,

but before long she will meet him in that land of bliss where parting will be no more forever. Capt. Branom was a very remarkable man. To write of the personal sacrifices, the trials and disappointments he has suffered and endured for his country's interest would moisten the cheeks of every reader of this history. Hundreds of illustrations could be given, strikingly demonstrative of this fact, but space forbids. When Capt. Branom came to Texas, a mere lad, it is said a single glance at his splendid presence won every heart, and the whole people took him on trust. Be it said to the credit of this grand old pioneer he never betrayed the trust, would have suffered the tortures of a cruel death first, always was reliable and could be depended upon in the midst of storms.

BIOGRAPHY OF R. LINDLEY.

R. Lindley was born in Polk County, Missouri in the year 1835. He migrated to Hopkins County with his father Jahu Lindley in 1849 and located on South Sulphur Creek where he was living when he died. Jahu Lindley had a large family but there are only two of this family living at this time: the subject of this biographical sketch and R. J. Lindley, who lives in Decatur, Wise County, at this time. R. Lindley was raised in Hopkins County. At the age of 23 years he married Miss Effie Sayle of Commerce, Hunt County, a lady of excellent birth and splendid ancestry. By this

union 7 children were born to them, two of these
are dead. Mr. Lindley has given two of his sons
professions and they are located in business and
are doing well, one son Jahu lives in the county
and is a prosperous well to do farmer and stock
raiser, a heavy tax payer and a splendid citizen,
reliable, just, honest, in fact he is a superb gentleman any where he is met. Mr. Lindley began
life with no capital save energy and a determina-
tion to succeed, he has made life a success and
to-day is considered one of the heaviest tax payers
of Hopkins County. He has been liberal with his
children, assisting them in many ways. He has
large stock interests in the county, and spends his
time in looking after and watching over his affairs.
He advocates schools and supports them liberally.
He is an honest man in all his dealings and is looked
upon as a first rate business man.

BIOGRAPHY OF J. R. LINDLEY.

J. R. Lindley was born in the state of Kentucky,
in the year of 1824. His parents moved into
Dade County, Missouri, in the year 1835 when
J. R. was only 11 years of age, where he grew up
into manhood. Filled with the spirit of adventure
and fired by the stories of the wealth of California,
he made an overland trip to the Pacific Coast in
the year of 1850, traveling with an ox train and
being four months on the road. He remained on
the Pacific slope for three years, returning to

Missouri he engaged in driving stock from Arkansas to the state of Kansas. He was a soldier in the Confederate Army and served under that entrepid soldier Gen. Joe Shelby and took part in many thrilling engagements in the war. He settled in Hopkins County after the war was ended. He owns large tracts of land and cattle on many hills and valleys. By reason of ownership he is enabled to pasture his cattle and his mules upon his own possession. He married Miss Emily daughter of David Rountree of Missouri. Ten children were born to this marriage. Their names and order of birth are: John D., a bachelor, who by the practice of rigid economy has amassed a small fortune; Addie is the wife of Edwin Brooks, a kindly disposed prosperous citizen of the county; Joseph Sidney married Miss Gafford, daughter of Thomas Gafford; Miss Florence married John N. Cox, a gentleman of noble birth who will be most pleasantly remembered for many years as the big hearted county clerk of Hopkins County. They have only one child, a daughter, Miss Myrtle, whom they are giving every advantage; James C. is also a bachelor, and is succeeding quite well; Miss Bettie is single and lives at home with her parents, she has many friends and is quite popular in society circles; Miss Ruthie married Dr. W. E. Kennemur, a young physician of scientific attainments being admirably fitted for the profession he is prompt and systematic in his habits, neat with his work, kind and obliging in disposition. Leonidas is dead. Miss

Mattie married Lee Bridges, an industrious, per-
severing business young man of good blood, the
name Bridges has ever been prominent in the county.
Miss Pearl is a nice, sweet young lady, possessed
to amiable qualities and a lovable disposition.
Mr. Lindley is a zealous member of the Christian
Church and an ardent Sunday school man.   He
takes pleasure in relating an amusing incident that
occurred with himself and a negro boy in an early
day near Sulphur Creek bottom.   He had a lot of
cattle that from neglect had become wild and were
unmanageable.   On this occassion he took this
negro with him to hunt up one of the wild animals
and slaughter it for beef.   They found the cattle
and shot one of the largest in the flank so as to
wound it in such a manner as to be able to secure
it.   In driving the wounded steer out of the dense
thicket to an open point in the timber, it showed
a disposition to sulk; the negro dismounted, leading
his horse and attempted to drive it on foot, the
animal stopped under the shade of a large oak
tree and as the negro advanced upon the steer,
in the twinkling of an eye, like the crack of doom,
the ox sprang with all the ferociousness of a tiger
upon the horse, killing him instantly and although the negro was well armed he cast his arms
away and ran for a sapling hard by.   He had just
gotten out of reach of the steer when he lunged
with all the power and force that was in him against
the small tree and broke it off at the root, it fell
and lodged in the forks of a small bois'd'arc tree.

The negro hanging on to the falling tree frightened and alarmed out of his senses, Mr. Lindley heard a muffled voice in the distant which sounded lonely, sad and melancholy, it was the negro repeating the words: "Oh Lord have mercy, Oh Lord God, Lordee, Oh Lord, Oh Mr. Lindley do run here." Mr. Lindley ran with all possible haste and shot the brute dead, the negro was relieved but it is said that he turned gray by the next morning.

BIOGRAPHY OF FRED W. CONLY.

Fred W. Conly was born in the state of North Carolina, August 29th, 1828. His father moved to Georgia when he was an infant three year old. He grew into manhood in the state of Georgia, and came to the state of Texas in the year 1852, and stopped in Cass County, where he met Miss Zilpha Peacock, won her affections and married her in the year 1857. By this union one child was born. This wife died very soon, and he afterwards married Miss Mary Hancock and moved into Hopkins County where he has resided ever since. By this marriage seven children were born, only four of this number are living in the county. His boys are all farmers. His second companion passed away and he subsequently married the sister of his last wife, another Miss Hancock. This wife still lives. By this marriage three children came to them, two of these are living, they live with their parents. He has led a useful life, and is postmaster at Evans Point. He is an honest, just and truthful man. He is a member of the Methodist Church and has lived a devout Christian for 40 years. He is liberal in his views, consistent in his actions. He is 74 years old, in poor health, is weakly, and complains of feebleness.

BIOGRAPHY OF W. M. HOGSETT.

W. M. Hogsett was born in the state of Tennessee on the 22nd day of February 1835. At the age of sixteen years he came to Texas with his mother and located near the old Lollar store. His father was a soldier in the Mexican war and died in the year 1846, while he was serving his country as a soldier. At the age of 21 years Mr. Hogsett married Miss Elizabeth Liles, daughter of William Liles then of Sulphur Springs and began to battle with the question of bread and butter. By this union five children were born, only one of these is living, Amos Hogsett. Mr. Hogsett lost his first companion and subsequently married Melvina Voss, and were the parents of six children, four of these are living. They all reside in the county, only one living at home, Miss Pearl, a bright intellectual woman of engaging manners and social disposition. Mr. Hogsett is living at this time near where his mother located when he was a child. He has farmed and raised stock for a livelihood. Some years ago he diverted his attention to the raising of blooded horses and mules. He has handled some of the best blooded animals, perhaps, that have ever been imported into the county. His name is familiar to every old citizen of the county as a stock man and as an active, energetic and industrious citizen. He has lived a life time as a friend and neighbor of Sealin Stout, who was the champion bear hunter in an early day in the county. They have passed many hours fire hunting at night. It was said of Mr. Stout when he saw the eye of the animal or beast of his search, that he could invariably determine the position of the body by the movements of the eye. He used a flint and steel rifle and was successful in securing his game. He kept a trained slow track dog upon which he relied, and it is said that his faithful dog never deceived his master. On one occasion this dog barked all night at a tree in the woods near by, when visited next morning by Mr. Stout it proved to be a bee tree. Mr. Hogsett relates an interesting love affair that came near annihilating the woman who figured so conspiciously in the matter and proved disastrous to the two gentlemen interested in this remarkable circumstance. A Mr. B. and Mr. L., became enamored of the same lady. She was beautiful in face and form, of good family and blood and a belle in her day. She was engaged to marry Mr. L., who was a violinist and a lover of his bottle. She loved him, and lavished her affections upon him without stint or limit, and was never happy only when she was in his company. In fact she centered her affections upon Mr. L.

with all the ardency that only woman is capable of bestowing. She knew full well, that this ardency of affections was reciprocated and that she had her share of his affections. Mr. B. loved her perhaps as devotedly and as sincerely as Mr. L., as the reader will soon know. While Mr. L. was engaged in playing the fiddle for a ball in old Tarrant, which was given at night time, Mr. B. rode to the home of the young woman and stole her away from her father's house, osensibly to marry Mr. L., and carried her to the home of Mr. Hogsett. Mr. L., who was entirely ignorant of all this proceedings and stratagem did not come of course. The next morning she persuaded Mr. B. to go in search of her absent and derelict lover. When he returned he informed the dispairing woman that her lover was beastly drunk and in no condition to marry. With her happy anticipations blasted, her home forsaken, and almost broken hearted she fell upon her knees and offered up a pitiful and heartfeeling petition to the God of heaven to guide and direct her in this hour of her greatest need. When this prayer was over Mr. B. said with emphasis: "Marry me, I love you, and shall protect, stand by and defend you." She accepted his proposition in the midst of tears and they were married. Mr. L., upon hearing of this dextrous and artful stratagem upon the part of Mr. B., became indignant and sought to take the life of Mr. B. They subsequently became friends, Mr. B. died, and Mr. L. married the widow. Mr. L. lived but a short time.

He fell from his horse between Sulphur Springs and Black Jack Grove and froze to death.

BIOGRAPHY OF FRANK PIERCE.

Frank Pierce is an old time citizen of Hopkins County, he came into the county in the early forties. He married Miss South at an early day and reared a large family in Hopkins County. This family was unfortunate and died in early life. J. K. Pierce, a prosperous farmer and stock raiser and a wealthy citizen of the county, is his son. Frank Pierce Jr. is another son. They had different mothers. In the year of 1848 Frank Pierce was a member of the Grand Jury, during the sitting of the District Court at old Tarrant, John T. Mills presiding Judge. The court house was built of logs and the Grand Jury occupied a small log cabin which was built of poles upon the banks of a little dry branch some three hundred yards east from the court house building. Eldridge Hopkins, who was county clerk, ran a boarding house; this house consisted of a couple of log cabins with hall and piazza on either side. The Grand Jury, the judge and attorneys boarded with Mr. Hopkins during the sitting of the court. The Grand Jury was composed of Harry Hargrave, Frank Pierce, Carroll Crisp, Joe Salmon, Harry Hopkins, the names of the other members of this body have passed from the mind of Mr. Pierce. The planks that were placed upon the sleepers of Mr. Hopkins cabin

hotel were not confined by nails. He accommodat-
ed all the court and some of their wives to lodging,
and was a jolly good fellow. The judge convened
court on Monday and dismissed it on the following
Saturday at twelve o'clock. There were no convictions, no bills of indictment found. When the
jury was discharged and court adjourned, the jury
was paid for their services in county script, which
Mr. Hopkins accepted in payment for board. Only
one incident transpired during the sitting of this
court that is worthy of record. Col. Bill Young,
prosecuting attorney, and Brad Fowler indulged
too freely during the week and got on a high lone-
some. They, too, boarded at Eldridge Hopkins'
hotel. When these two gentlemen became too gay
and hilarious, Mr. Hopkins in a persuasive and
kindly manner asked them to respect his guests.
One night in the week Col. Young secured a pair
of Texas cow boy spurs, these spurs were profusely
and lavishly belled. He arranged with Brad
Fowler that he place himself in the position of a
horse, and he would ride him over the hotel floor.
This feat was performed in the still hours of the
night. When Fowler began to pitch, in imitation
of a mustang horse, the bells upon the spurs began
to tinkle, the loose plank in the floor began to
rattle, and Young hallowing " Woah, woah, woah,"
a noise fell upon the ears of the inmates like the
crack of doom and frightened them, men and women,
almost senseless. It appeared to the inmates of
the hotel that his satanic majesty with all of his

imps had come upon them with the fury of a tornado and that destruction and devastation was upon them. Men and women left their beds and pallets and sought safety in the open air. When the excitement and alarm was over and it was ascertained that the trick was all a joke, the guests returned to their sleeping quarters and rested till day. This incident was a subject of talk for months after.

There was one whiskey house in the village of Tarrant, owned and run by Tom Louden, tin cups were used for glasses, and gourds for dippers. When court adjourned each juryman bought a Spanish gourd of whiskey, hung the gourd by means of a raw hide string tied around its center to the horn of the saddle, and hied himself to his home. The refined and delicate feeling of the reader may be shocked at the foregoing incident. This is an occurrence of real life, and the actors of this scene have long since passed from the stage of life, gone to learn the dread reality of an unknown world. When God lays his hands upon a man the world should let him rest. No more will we hear of the actions of these men until we all meet on eternity's wave, beyond death's chilling flood, to enjoy the association of the angels of heaven in eternity.

Justice and mercy should be our motto, these words should be inscribed upon our banner. We plead for our fellow human, a greater charity from those who would sit in judgment. The greatest men and the greatest minds have long since recognized that what those of a lesser would call vices, are really diseases of the mind and body, afflictions that need our tenderest pity and sympathy and which is our duty to alleviate as far as lies in our power, by that humane fellow-feeling, which makes the whole world a kin. The whole philosophy of life consists in knowing what is true in order to do what is right. Every good act is charity. Exhortation to another to do right is charity. A man's true wealth hereafter is the good he has done in this world to his fellow man.

BIOGRAPHY OF THE WAGGONERS.

Luth Waggoner was born in the state of Missouri in the year 1833, and moved with his parents in the year 1839 to Red River District, Texas, and stopped where Blossom Prairie is located. The family remained there and farmed and raised stock for a period of ten years, and moved to Hopkins County where L. Waggoner has lived all his life. Luth's father, Solomon Waggoner, had a large family when they came into Hopkins County. There are only two of this family living in Hopkins County at this time, Luth and N. B. Waggoner. Luth married Miss Nancy Millsap at the age of twenty one years, a daughter of Jacob Millsap, an old time Texan. To this union four children were born. One of these is living in Hopkins County, Rufus, a planter, a splendid citizen, and enjoys the respect and confidence of all who know him. Luth Waggoner has engaged in agricultural pursuits and stock raising, has devoted his time to this business and has been reasonably successful. He has suffered some serious and severe losses. He lost his first companion, and subsequently married Miss Louise Forbus. This union has been a happy one. They have raised a large and interesting family of bright children—of manly men and womanly women. Two of his daughters have married and are among the best class of citizens in the county. Luther is a sincere, conscientious, God-serving man, honest and just in all the relations of life, and has a heart full of charity. He saw hard service in the Civil war. He volunteered in Hopkins County and entered the service in the Twenty-third Texas Cavalry, Gould's Regiment, and served during the war. He returned at the close of the war and began life over. Soon a dark cloud overshadowed him—the loss of his companion. This calamity was a great shock to Mr. Waggoner, and brought financial ruin upon him. He is a zealous member of the Baptist church, and has been for twenty-five years. He is now an old man and in feeble health, and feels that his days here on earth are few. N. B. Waggoner is a native Texan, born in Red River County, and has lived in Hopkins County all his life. When he grew up into manhood he married Miss Lucy Crisp, daughter of Uncle Carroll Crisp, an old pioneer citizen of Hopkins County. Uncle Carroll was famous for his great liberality and generosity.

His unbounded hospitality gathered around him many friends, and his numerous acts of kindness will long be remembered by those who were the beneficiaries. Kind and noble-hearted Uncle Carroll Crisp has left behind him "footprints on the sands of time." Mr. Waggoner and his wife have raised only one child, a daughter. She has been twice married, and lives near her parents with her second companion. Mr. Waggoner has been successful in accumulating property. He is a member of the Baptist church. His membership is at Pleasant Grove, a beautiful country church, situated in the heart of one of the most prosperous neighborhoods in the county. Its membership consists of some of the most refined and substantial citizens of the county. James R. Beck, Sid Lackey, Zack Bailey and other prominent men in the county are members of this church. Bro. Gaddy is their pastor, a splendid gentleman and a great gospel preacher. A man's true wealth hereafter is the good he has done in this world to his fellow man. When he dies the people will ask what property he has left behind him, but the angels will ask what good deeds has he sent on before him.

BIOGRAPHY OF THE WEAVERS.

Green Weaver, deceased, moved with his family into Hopkins County in the year 1845 and located in the vicinity of where Greenview Church is now situated. He is the father of two sets of children, having been twice married. His first set of children were notorious for the brilliancy of their intellect. They are all dead now. Mrs. Mary J. Moseley is the eldest child of the second marriage, Sam Houston Weaver, who is a well-known, respected and esteemed citizen of the county, is his second child, and lives at this time on his father's head-right. Sam is a highly respected citizen, having raised a large and useful family in the county. Dave W. lives in Eastland County. Granville lives in Lebanon, Indian Territory. Walton is now living in Oklahoma Territory. Joe Weaver lives at his father's old home. These children are all good, useful citizens, honest and just men, and go to make much of the history of Hopkins County. They too have suffered, in common with other pioneers, the trials, hardships, disappointments and self-sacrifices attendant upon pioneer life in the county. They are an honor and credit to the state as well as to the county, having been born and raised in the county.

BIOGRAPHY OF MILLER GREEN.

Miller Green, who lives at Black Jack Grove, is a native Texan. He was born in Red River district in the year 1837. Two years after his birth his father moved into the vicinity of where Greenville in Hunt County is situated. In the year 1854 he moved to where he is now living. In the year 1867 Miller married Ophelia Cole, daughter of Wash Cole, an old pioneer and one of the first who came to Hopkins County. He was highly respected and esteemed by all of his acquaintances. His name is agreeably remembered as that of one of the leading personages of the county. Ophelia was born at Old Sulphur Bluff in the year 1845, She is dead now, and so is her father. Miller Green has seven children living. He was a Texas Ranger, and served his state as an Indian fighter for two years. He was a soldier in the Confederate army and saw hard service for four years. He served under General Ross in the Ninth Texas Cavalry, receiving a slight wound while in the discharge of his duty. When he returned from the war he engaged in farming and stock raising, and was reasonably successful. He has always been in easy circumstances, meeting his obligations promptly. He has been a taxpayer in the county since and before his majority. He has encouraged the upbuilding of schools, and has been liberal in their support. He is ready at all times to give encouragement to any enterprise for the improvement of his community, a good citizen, a debt-paying man and a Democrat.

BIOGRAPHY OF DR. R. C. HOLDERNESS.

Dr. R. C. Holderness was born in the state of North Carolina in the year 1827. In the year 1850 he graduated in medicine from the University of Pennsylvania, and subsequently moved to the state of Arkansas, Calhoun County, where he began the successful practice he has always enjoyed. In the year 1863 he migrated to Hopkins County, where he has lived since in the enjoyment of a lucrative practice. The doctor married Miss Virginia Thomas, an old Carolina lady, in the state of Arkansas. They both came from the same county in North Carolina and migrated to the same county in Arkansas. They were united in marriage in the year 1854. Ten children were born to this union, five sons and five daughters. Four of these were born in Arkansas. Nine of his children are living; only two single, who live with their aged father in Cumby. His companion died in the year 1894, and is laid away in the cemetery in Cumby. She was a Christian lady, and practiced her religion in all the walks of life; a devoted mother and an affectionate wife. Dr. Holderness has ever taken great interest in public enterprises and has contributed his time and money to aid in the completion of them. He is a cool-headed man of fine judgment. The social position of his family is equal to any in the state, and the doctor is a polished gentleman. He is an ardent supporter of Christianity, being a member of the Methodist church, and has acted as steward in this church for fifty-two years. He was converted in Arkansas. He has ever been a man of good habits, using neither spirits nor tobacco in any form. He is a hale hearty fellow. His step is elastic and his form erect, although he is burdened with the weight of seventy-five years. He attributes his physical condition to his abstemious habits.

BIOGRAPHY OF THE SPARKS FAMILY.

James B. Sparks, deceased, father of W. J., John N. and A. W. Sparks and also the father of four daughters, came into Texas in the year 1851. He remained one year in the state and returned to his old home in the state of Alabama, and moved his family to the state of Texas in the fall of 1852. He settled on the county line separating Hopkins from Titus County, on the headwaters of Big Cypress Bayou. Mr. James Sparks' brothers had moved into the state of Texas as early as the year 1836, and settled on Cypress Bayou near Cypress Church, where they had engaged in farming and raising stock. They built the first gin house that was anywhere to be seen in all the country for miles around.

A. W. Sparks was only nine years old when his father came with his family to his Texas home. His business was to look after the stock and to work on the plantation. As the country began to increase in numbers, the people commenced to erect church buildings and school houses. When schools could be had the Sparks children had the benefit of them, as their father was an ardent advocate of learning, and sought every opportunity possible to give his children a common-sense, practical education. W. J. Sparks, the oldest son, was a printer and worked at Henderson, Texas, on a newspaper called the "Flag of the Union." On the death of the editor of the "Flag" Mr. Sparks had full control of the management of the paper. This was during the year 1854, before he had attained his majority. He subsequently established a newspaper in the town of Quitman, in Wood County. He finally read law, and became a prominent attorney, and practiced his profession in the courts of Hopkins County for a long while, and then moved west and died. John N. Sparks has been a citizen of Hopkins County almost continuously since childhood, and is living in the county at this time. He is well known as a stock man and as a sheep raiser. He has raised a large family of healthy, intelligent children. His daughters have married Hopkins County boys, all of whom are of splendid blood and ancestry, and are doing well. Dr. Buck Sparks is his son; a young physician of more than ordinary ability, possessed of great energy and ambition. John N. Sparks is a heavy taxpayer in the county. The entire Sparks family espoused the Southern cause and were Confederate soldiers, and served as such throughout the war. Many of them had seen service in the Indian war. When A. W. Sparks returned from the Civil war he met Miss Fannie Turner, whom he soon married, obtaining his license to wed from Zeph Matthews, at old Tarrant. This marriage has proven to be a physiological one. Three children having been born to them, all of whom are possessed of gentle manners and a kindly disposition. They are all married now, and have homes of their own. Mr. Sparks has been engaged in school teaching, in agricultural pursuits and in stock raising. He has ideality large, and is fond of the lovely and beautiful. Accompanying these traits of character he has literary taste and attainment, and is the author of an interesting history of the war between the states. He has written many articles of interest to the public. He is now carrying the weight of sixty-one years; is active, supple and strong, and bids fair to live to a great age. He is well-informed upon the general topics, such as church, politics, social and business matters. He enjoys the confidence of the people, and is an honest, reliable and trustworthy citizen of the county. He is abreast of the times. His writings are sought after by the reading public. Being of an analytical mind, he condenses without padding, writes from a human stand-point, and places his soul in what he writes. He has been a member of the Baptist church for a number of years. Also an enthusiastic member of the Masonic Fraternity.

BIOGRAPHY OF ROBERT ODOM.

Robert Odom was born in the state of Tennessee in the year 1846, and emigrated to Hopkins County with his father in the year 1850. His father, Jesse Odom, settled nineteen miles southeast of

Sulphur Springs and four miles west of Winsboro. The county was new and uninhabited, therefore Robert had not educational training. Growing up amid the wilds of the country, he was surrounded with all the environments common to a pioneer life. At the age of twenty-two years he met Miss Lucinda Lambdin, a Texas girl who was visiting friends in Mr. Odom's section. He became attached to her at sight, and the result was marriage.

By this union eight children were born to them. They are all living at this time. Six of them are married and live in Hopkins County. Mr. Odom now lives near Cumby, old Black Jack Grove. Lynch is his postoffice address. He is a well-known and useful citizen of the county. He is a zealous and ardent advocate of education. Having been denied the benefit of educational advantages, he has studiously sought and striven to educate those dependent upon him. Therefore he has been a strong supporter of schools in every way possible. He and his family are members of the Presbyterian church. He has ever been moral, and religiously inclined, and has set this example through life. He is a kind-hearted, sympathetic gentleman and has the full confidence of all who know him. He relates an incident of a great revival of religion away back in the early fifties. This revival took place on the exact spot where Charley Taylor's residence is located. Rev. Johnson, a Methodist circuit rider, from Upsher County, in passing the home of Mr. Odom's father, left an

appointment to preach at a given time. Young
Odom and a companion were sent out in all directions to inform the settlers of the appointment.
The meeting continued for eleven days with aston-
ishing results. Ben Elder, a Baptist minister,
aided Rev. Johnson in conducting the services.
The outgrowth of this great revival was the upbuilding of the County Line Church, situated a
couple of miles south of where this meeting was
held. The people gathered from all directions
and all sections of the country. They came in
ox carts, in wagons, on horseback and on foot.
Rev. Johnson closed an unusually solemn sermon
with a powerful exhortation to every one present
who wanted to escape hell and the awful groans
and screams of the damned that were then burning
in hell fire, and who wanted to meet him in heaven,
to signify it by a clap of the hands and a shout of
glory. It is said that when the signal was given
the clap of hands and shout of glory sounded like
a thunder bolt and was loud enough to waken the
dead. This scene beggars description. The con-
fusion and the great noise stampeded the horses and
the oxen, put the dogs to fighting, and frightened
what few negroes were present out of their wits.
The negroes said: "De world is shore comin' to de
end; let us all pray too."

Preachers and people evidently believed in the
reality of heaven and hell, and showed their faith
by their works. There was no such thing as playing at religion with them. Whether a man shouted,

danced, jumped, jerked or laughed in these religious exercises, it was the work of the Holy Spirit in him. The man who doubted that such things were produced by the Holy Spirit simply had to be close mouthed or he would be ostracised from society, abused by the preachers and bitterly persecuted by the whole country. How different in this day! People give close attention to what the preachers say, and care nothing for their actions in the pulpit. People are calling for less sounds and more sense from their preachers: more mind and less muscle, in this day and generation. Such songs as "I'm on my Journey Home," "Lord, I want more religion," do not have that electrical effect on an audience in this day of scientific thought, reading and understanding that they did fifty years ago. People do not suffer their emotions to overflow like an artesian well as of yore. They have learned that the application of common sense to all things pertaining to religious matters is the most effective and beneficial in the end.

Mr. Odom is not responsible for a part of the foregoing statement.

BIOGRAPHY OF G. W. HARPER, DECEASED.

Mr. Harper came to Hopkins County when he was quite a young man, although he had a wife and child. He located on a tract of land where he lived all his life. He was very unfortunate in his married life, having lost three companions during his life. There were twenty-one children born to these three marriages. Out of this large number only three are living. Miss Minerva, the eldest daughter, married Lodwick Vaden, Jr., and lives upon one of the most fertile plantations on South Sulphur Creek. They have a nice, growing family of bright, intellectual children. He and his companion are both active members of the Christian church, and their walk and conversation attest the sincerity of their faith, and their lively appreciation of what it teaches. He is deservedly very popular in the county, and the number of his friends is limited only by the number of his acquaintances. Miss Mattie married John S. Chapman, a gentleman whom to know is to love, They have a small family of bright, industrious children, whom he is educating in books and in agricultural pursuits as well. They have one daughter married, Miss Pru, a nice, sweet woman, who is the wife of James Chapman, a distant relative. They live near their parents. Mr. John Chapman is a heavy taxpayer in the county. A. S. Harper married Josephine Pruitt, a beautiful lady of splendid family, and lives on his father's old homestead. He is living a moral, upright life, thoroughly correct in all his habits. He was always impressed that the confidence of others was a strong element of success, and that the only way to possess it was to truly merit it. Miss Alice, a most estimable young woman married John Knox, Esq., a prominent gentleman and a justice of the peace. He has education sufficient to give him position and standing in the community, He leads a quiet and exemplary life, devoted to his home affairs and the duty of his office.

BIOGRAPHY OF SERENA MILLHOLLIN.

Serena Millhollin, a daughter of Sam Lindley, known all over Hopkins County as Aunt Serena, gives a graphic account of pioneer life in Hopkins County. She says: "My father was born in the state of Kentucky, and married my mother in the state of Arkansas, and then migrated to the Republic of Mexico and stopped on North Sulphur Creek. [By reference to the first chapter in this history the reader will notice that the territory of Texas once belonged to Mexico.] about where the village of Ben Franklin is located, and remained for only one year and then moved to South Sulphur Creek, where he located for life. My mother's maiden name was Letha Turmon. My father lived to be eighty-three years old. My mother survived him a few years and then passed to her reward. There were six children born to them. Five of these are living. Serena married Jacob Millhollin at the age of fifteen years. Jacob was a good, inoffensive, uneducated, honest man. Bartholomew married Lavina Jackson. He is a farmer and stock man, Jordina married Wig Collins, brother to Red Collins. She lived but a short

time. Alice married Aiden Posey, a big-hearted
fellow of splendid blood, a gentleman whom every
one respects. Lethia married Bat Millhollin, a
gentleman of noble parts, genial and social to an
eminent degree." Aunt Serena is now sixty-six
years old. When her father moved into the neighborhood where she is now living she was only seven
years old, but she recollects distinctly the cabin
her father built on the spot she was raised. It
was built of logs and covered with clapboards.
In size it was 14x14 feet with only one opening
and a dirt floor. It was erected in the brush near
Sulphur Creek. Cooking was performed under a
brush or pole arbor. Water was brought from
Sulphur Creek in small kegs on horseback. It
was made her duty to go twice every day to the
creek after water, carrying with her for company
her little brother Bartholomew. Corn meal was
produced in the manner hitherto described in this
history. "My parents had all of their children
come into the cabin at twilight every evening—the
lights all extinguished—and there in the cabin
we all sat till bedtime, not speaking except in a
low whisper. This state of affairs continued for
about four years. A dark, lonely time we all
experienced during all these long years. Could
the reader but know and feel as we knew and felt
in those dark and gloomy times, he would better
appreciate his happy surroundings. There in that
lonely hut in the dense wild woods, we have lain
all the dark and gloomy night, cringing and shiv-

ering from every noise without, not knowing at
what moment we would all be massacred by the
savage Indians, who were all around in the brush.
Dear reader, pause for one moment and go back
sixty years with me to the days of my innocent
childhood, placing yourself in my helpless and
lonely condition. To-day, as this grand old
pioneer lady walks the streets of her country town
and remembers when the Indians roamed its vir-
ginal wilds, when the bears and panthers inhabited
its dense thickets, where the wild cats screamed
and the catamount cried, accompanied with the
solemn and lonely chanting of the whippoorwill
solo, and hears her dress criticised and her personal appearance discussed, her heart is saddened
within her. People who indulge in sport of this
character should be taken up by the law and sent
to some institution for the feeble minded. Were
the author familiar with the names of such persons
he would not soil and befoul the pages of this history by personal reference. In the language of
the great Solomon, "A fool is joined to his folly,"
but fortunately it is said that the God of heaven
has wisely made provision for fools and idiots.

BIOGRAPHY OF THE ELI LINDLEY FAMILY.

John W. Lindley, elder son of Eli Lindley, deceased,
gives this thrilling and graphic account of many incidents that occurred within his recollection during
his father's life in Hopkins County. He remem-

bers quite distinctly when his father came into the
territory of Hopkins County. J. W. Lindley is sixty-
three years of age. He married Miss Nancy Rea, sister
to Neal Rea, at the termination of the Civil war. He
has raised a large family of healthy children who are
respected citizens of the county. Jacob Marion,
a prominent business man of Peerless, is his oldest
son. Uncle Eli Lindley married Sallie Crisp in
the state of Missouri. Aunt Sallie, as she was
called (her name being synonymous with everything that was kind and good), has gone from us
now. Aunt Sallie and Uncle Eli were the parents
of seventeen children. Five of this number died
in infancy. Jacob M. married Miss Jo Crutchfield,
She died and he married Miss Starkey Houston
and shortly afterwards he passed to his eternal
home. Green died while a student at McKenzie
College in Red River County. Elizabeth married
Harry Portwood. By this union two children
were born to them. Harry died and Lizzie married
Clabe Gates, with whom she is living at this time
in Decatur County. Jonathan and Amanda were
twins. Jonathan married Miss Hughes. She lived
only a short while and he subsequently married
Miss Mattie Cobb, a lady of excellent family and
splendid ancestry, they have a large and interesting
family. Amanda married Marshall Lindley, a distant
relative. Some of their offspring are citizens of the
county and are respected and esteemed for their
real worth. Eli F., a prominent gin man and an
all around business man, married Miss Victoria

Bailey, a daughter of an old pioneer Texan. They have a nice young family of boys and girls. Miss Josephine married James Crowder, a stepson of Volney Rattan of Delta County. A great calamity befell Mrs. Crowder in the untimely death of her husband a few years back. She has four children, two girls and two boys. She is very much interested in the correct training and educating of her children, believing that to educate means to become useful citizens, and that knowledge is power. Mrs. Josephine lives in Cooper now, and is a prosperous business lady of the town. Miss Sallie is a beautiful blonde, and an accomplished and polished young lady, possessed of engaging manners. Miss Mary is a sweet girl of domestic habits. Her ideality is large and she is unexcelled in her needle work. Mary Ellen Lindley married Jack Worsham, a man possessed of a large share of common sense. He has been successful in business, the result of his own energy, foresight and good judgment. He bears an enviable reputation throughout the county. They have five children—three boys and two girls. An unfortunate and grievous accident befell his family a short time since in the explosion of a coal-oil lamp, which resulted in the death of one of his daughters. Miss Docia married Mr. John Jordon, a son of an old pioneer citizen of the county. Mr. Jordon is an honest, upright gentle-man, a farmer and a successful stock-raiser. They have raised a nice family. His daughters are all beautiful, nice and neat. Some of them are married and have done well in their selection of husbands. Jefferson Davis Lindley married Miss Dora Bailey, sister to his brother Eli's wife. Jeff is a successful stock-raiser and planter, a good, worthy, upright citizen of the county. They have five children. One of their daughters is married. Their eldest daughter, Miss Mary Ellen, is a reigning belle, and her association is sought after by the best young people of the county. Her parents are endeavoring to give her a finished education, which Miss Ellen encourages and appreciates. Jeff is the youngest child of the seventeen and is named in honor of Jefferson Davis of Confederate fame. Uncle Eli Lindley reared this large family on South Sulphur Creek, where he moved sixty years ago. This family has passed through all the hardships attendant upon pioneer life. The water that this family used in an early day was hauled from holes in Sulphur Creek in wooden vessels, upon slides drawn by one or two oxen. Gourds (when they could be obtained) were used for many purposes: water gourds, milk gourds, honey gourds, sugar gourds, fat gourds. A gourd with a long neck was used as a funnel—a pipe or passage for conducting liquids into other vessels. When gourds could not be obtained, buffalo horns were brought into requisition, and were made to answer the same purposes as the gourds. In many instances holes were pored into the rough, improvised dining table and buffalo horns were introduced and used instead of dippers or cups.

At one time when neither gourds nor buffalo horns could be had, the clapper was removed from a large cow-bell and the bell was used as a gourd. The bell was passed around with pioneer hospitality. The visitor was asked to have a bell of water. In the absence of suitable vessels deer-skins were cased from the carcass and the legs of the skin were tied together. This hide then formed a sack in which many articles were conveyed from place to place, such as corn, peas, lard and honey. When meal could not be obtained the breast of wild turkey was dried and used for bread. Venison was also used in the same manner as the turkey bread. When bear was killed the flesh was called meat, and hog flesh was called meat; but venison and turkey were called bread. Deer were so plentiful that J. W. Lindley, with a hired hand, stood upon one spot and killed seven at one time. The whole country was literally over-run with wild animals. The mustang roamed the country in droves, and were a source of much annoyance to the settlers.

BIOGRAPHY OF THOS. S. GLOVER.

Thos. S. Glover was born in Troupe County, Georgia, in the year 1836, and migrated with his parents to the state of Mississippi. When only a boy he came to Texas with his uncle William Glover in the year 1845, and stopped for a time in Harrison County, and in the fall of the same year moved to Hopkins County. Thomas was only ten years of age at this time. They settled near where the old town of Tarrant was located. Mr. Glover relates many incidents of early life in Texas. It was at this old town that he first met Miss Ruth Lindley, a daughter of Uncle Eli and Sallie Lindley. Their first meeting was attended with some romance. An acquaintance was cultivated, which resulted in their marriage. From this union fourteen children were born, eleven are living. They are six girls and five boys. Five of these children are living at the home of their parents. They are all healthy, well born children. When Mr. Glover came into Hopkins County it was almost an uninhabited wilderness. But little attention was given to the law, though there was an organized court held at the county site. The pioneer citizens had no patience with thieves, thugs and evil doers. When a horse-thief was caught stealing or in possession of property not his own, no redress was sought by the law. He was immediately swung up on the most convenient limb, and that was the last of the transaction. They stole no more, of course. The author has seen three horse-thieves, each minus one ear, hanging to one huge tree in a deep forest growth. This gruesome sight was not pleasant to behold. Every citizen was a law unto himself. The bowie knife and pistol were his body guards. These weapons were a part of his dress, and nearly all disputes were settled by one or the other of them. Men had to be men and stand up like men among men. A coward was not recognized by the ladies, but a man was rewarded and appreciated by them for brave and courageous deportment. William Glover had employed Mr. Fanning to haul a load of salt from Grand Saline. When the salt was delivered Glover paid Fanning for his services, and Fanning expressed satisfaction. Upon the return from a buffalo hunt in which they were all successful Mr. Fanning demanded more pay. Glover refused and attempted to reason with Fanning, but to no good effect. Fanning said: "My name, sir, is Hugh J. Fanning. I am a blood cousin to General Fanning of Alamo fame, and I fear no man on earth." Mr. Glover replied: "I am not related to General Fanning of Alamo fame, but, sir, I am not a coward when it becomes necessary for me to act in defense of what I know to be right." Fanning immediately left Glover and returned in the afternoon armed with a rifle gun, a six shooter and an ugly bowie knife. Mr. Glover was at his wagon with his family when Mr. Fanning came up. Mrs. Glover, observing Fanning's approach, ran to her husband's side and begged and prayed to Fanning not to kill her husband. Fanning walked coolly around the wagon in order to get a better view of his intended victim. During this time Glover had taken from the side of his wagon a single barrel flint and steel shot gun. Fanning shot at Glover, but missed his aim, his shot taking effect in the clothing of Mrs. Glover's infant child, which she had carried all this time in her arms. Quite a large hole was shot through the infant's clothing. Glover then shot, and killed Fanning on the spot. The last words he ever spoke were: "Bill, you have killed me." This incident occurred just across the county line and not in Hopkins County. Mr. Glover tells of an exciting bear chase in which Sam Bromley was sent for with his dogs—Old Trimbush and other dogs. The bear was caught, carried to old Tarrant, dressed, weighed and divided. It was the custom of the hunters to have the owners of the dogs fire the first shot. On this occasion this rule was violated, so the hunter who fired the first shot was called up to treat the entire crowd, which he did, the hunters filling their Spanish gourds with liquor, and going to their respective homes with bear meat and whisky.

Gip and Tom Glover are brothers and cousins to T. S. Glover. They are both good, worthy citizens who are highly respected and esteemed for their real worth. They have nice intelligent families, and are doing well.

BIOGRAPHY OF HAYWOOD MOONEY.

Haywood B. Mooney first saw the light of day in the state of Georgia, seventy-three years ago. His father moved to Alabama when Haywood was a child. When he had grown to be quite a lad, being rather precocious, he was stolen from his home and from his parents by sporting men who gambled on horse racing of fine blooded stock. They used him for light riding and he proved to be the very chap they needed in their profession, so they kept him for a period of three years by offering such inducements as would please the boy. About this time a war took place between the American Republic and the Republic of Mexico. Young Mooney was employed by the United States agent to carry the express mail from Mobile, Alabama, to Montgomery, Alabama. He continued in this capacity during the existence of the war. He then served as an apprentice and learned the trade of engineering and followed steamboating on the rivers for eight years. During this time his father had died and his mother had moved to Sulphur Springs, in Hopkins County, on what is known as the old Jim Mooney place. While Mr. Mooney was on his way to the county to see his aged mother, coming from Colorado River in Texas, where he had been engaged in steamboating for several years, he met Miss Martha Jane Goodson, the daughter of an esteemed old pioneer Texan, with whom he became attached. He returned to his labor on the river, but within one year's time he closed out the business of steamboating, visited his mother again, met once more the girl who had stolen his heart, and they were united in marriage. He and his bride left the state immediately and went by way of water to California. While in the state of California the Civil war be-

tween the states broke out. In order to prevent
the United States from conscripting him and com-
pelling him to serve in the Union army, he left
California with his family and moved to Oregon
and placed himself and family under the protection
of General Lane, a southern gentleman. When
the war was ended he went back to his home in
California and remained for a couple of years and
then returned to Hopkins County and settled upon
the exact spot of land where he has since lived and
raised his family. Haywood Jr. is his oldest
child. We give the name of his children and
their order of birth. Bill Mooney, Henry, Annie,
Sarah, Tom S., and Jim Mooney. They all live
within reach of their parents and are all good,
reliable, worthy citizens of the county. Mr. Mooney
is happily constituted. He is hopeful and very
cheerful. He has been a great dancer, and for
numbers of years has amused many in the performance of what is called in vulgar parlance
clog and jig dances. His family are all musicians,
and the Mooney band is famous in Hopkins County.
They are all sober, honest, upright men, but are
fond of much fun. Mr. Mooney has served his
county notably and honorably as deputy sheriff,
hunting up and running down horse-thieves and
other criminals and evil doers. He was looked
upon by this class of outlaws as being a terror to
them, and they always kept a close watch upon
his movements. He has been useful in many
ways. Being a born doctor he has been of great

help to his neighbors during sickness. Being
blessed with a kind heart and a generous disposition he has often been imposed upon by unap-
preciating people who would use his skill and medicine without compensating him.   He will be greatly
missed when he is called to his long home in eternity.

BIOGRAPHY OF REV. P. B. BAILEY.

Rev. P. B. Bailey, deceased, came to Texas
in the year 1845.   He became a citizen of Hopkins
County in the year 1850.   He was the father of
seven children.   These are all dead now but two—
Mrs. Mary Loving, mother of Wilber Loving, Hopkins County's efficient and popular sheriff, and
Mrs. M. E. Minter, wife of Capt. S. A. Minter,
who lives in the Pine Forest neighborhood.   He
was a Methodist preacher and organized the first
Methodist church that was ever established in
the town of Sulphur Springs.   The author has
heard this great preacher deliver powerful sermons.
He was a natural preacher.   He loved his work
intensely, and has been instrumental in converting
more people, perhaps, than any divine of his day.
His power of oratory was great, and when he became enthused, which he did with a full audience,
his efforts were stupendous.   On one occasion
when he had preached the funeral sermon of a
noble citizen of his acquaintance, he stepped from
the pulpit to the floor and began singing an ap-

propriate song, asking the audience to join in the singing. They were all too full. All tried to sing the song he had selected for the occasion, but failed. Women wept freely, old men and hardened sinners wept. Sobs and sighs burts from sorrow-burdened souls in all parts of the assembly. People fell into one anothers arms and sobbed as if their hearts would break, so powerful had been his exhortations while delivering his sermon. But the grand old preacher is dead now. When he passed away a deep gloom settled down upon the whole community. He died in 1873 at Rev. Lowe's residence in Sulphur Bluff. Thus passed away one of the most powerful gospel preachers of his day.

BIOGRAPHY OF THE OLDEST MAN IN THE COUNTY.

J. F. Youngblood is the oldest man living in Hopkins County. He was born in the year 1805, and is therefore ninety-seven years old. Tennessee is his native state. He came to Texas in the year 1848. He moved to Harrison County, but remained there only a short time. This was in the day of Regulators and Moderators. He has suffered great misfortunes, almost a calamity in his married life, having lost four companions. He is to-day living with his fifth wife. He has six children. Four of this number are living— Mrs. Hurley, mother of W. C. Hurley, postmaster

of Sulphur Springs, and John A. Hurley, a lawyer
of prominence in the county, Mrs. Ripley is another
daughter, a pure, good and noble woman, a widow,
who deserves great credit for the manner in which
she has raised her family. Mr. Youngblood has
been famous in three states as a singing teacher,
understanding the rudiments of music most thoroughly; and to-day, burdened as he is with the
weight of ninety-seven years, he can sing inter-
estingly and instructively. He has a mouth full
of good, sound teeth, having lost none of them
during his long life. He has never chewed or
smoked tobacco, has observed and practiced habits
of temperance, kept regular hours, spent his nights
at home with his family, and has lived a life of
personal purity. His religious views are somewhat
peculiar. He believes in an exclusive Christ,
Jesus is sovereign, universal king and only poten-
tate. He only is the Christ of God, he is the Saviour
of men, neither is there salvation in any other.
Being an Exclusivist he discards the beliefs of
sects and denominations. The Bible gives no
places for a plurality of brotherhood in Christ.
But one is your father and all ye are brethren.
One family in heaven and in earth. Eph. 3: 15.
For as we have many members in one body and
all members have not the same office, so we, being
many, are one body in Christ, and every one members one of another, only one body in Christ, as
we discern that body and know that God has in-
ducted us into the same, it were dishonesty in the

sight of God and a base, cowardly act to com-
promise to please men who admit several hundred
other bodies.

BIOGRAPHY OF G. L. STACY.

G. L. Stacy was born in Williamson County,
Tennessee, in the year 1825. He married Mary
Bell in his native state when he was twenty-two
years of age. In the year 1857 he came to Hopkins
County, and began the business of farming, and
has pursued this business all his life. Mr. Stacy
has five children living, three of whom live in Hopkins County. Lark, his oldest son, married Miss
Neely Earnest, the step-daughter of Dr. Stark,
a Baptist preacher; Miss Ellen married Mat Baker;
Miss Dollie married Eff Kimmins, and lived upon
their father's farm. Mr. Stacy has lived an exemplary life—sober, honest, industrious and just
in all the relations of life. He has accumulated
means sufficient to give his boys a good home,
which they appreciate. He has assisted his girls in
many ways. His companion, whom he married
at the age of sixteen, still lives to cheer and brighten
her husband in the declining days of his life. She
is hale and hearty, and presents the appearance of
one of long life. Very recently his sister who has
lived for a lifetime at the old Tennessee home
visited her brother in Hopkins County. The
brother and sister had not seen each other since
they separated at the old home, away back in
Tennessee, forty-nine years ago. Mr. Stacy did

not recognize his sister. Age had wrinkled her brow and furrowed her cheek, which was smooth and fair when they last saw each other. On recognizing his sister his emotions overcame him and he gave way to a flood of tears. She remained with her brother for a week and then returned to her home, which is now in Collin County, Texas. Mr. Stacy is a member of the Baptist church, and has lived a religious and consistent life. His family are members of the church of their father's choice, which is a source of much pleasure and satisfaction to their parents. Mr. Stacy has endeavored to use his talents in the interest of good morals and good citizenship. His home has been one of generosity and hospitality. His invitations to friends on public occasions are never limited. Everybody is welcome at his house, and all are aware of the fact. He has ever been ready to assist in any enterprise that would benefit his county, a liberal supporter of schools and other improvements for his neighborhood. He is seventy-eight years of age, and while the shadows are closing around him he feels that he has nothing to fear.

BIOGRAPHY OF REV. J. L. PRESTON.

Rev. Mr. Preston was born in the state of Tennessee in the year 1839. When he arrived at his majority he migrated to Tutis County, Texas, where he met Miss Mahala J. Caudle and they were united in marriage. He then moved to

Hopkins County. Eleven children were born to this union, eight of whom are living. They are all married, have homes and are doing well; being good, substantial citizens of the county. Their mother is a hale hearty woman, possessed of great energy and an amiable disposition. Dr. B. J. Preston, a young physician of prominence, and who passed away at Emblem in this county, was their son. Rev. Mr. Preston served as a soldier, acting as a non-commissioned officer in the war. He was a brave and courageous officer. He is a Baptist preacher, walking upright before God and man, has great force of character, his religion being of that practical kind which by act more than by word demonstrates the reality of his profession and the sincerity of his convictions. He is well and widely known in the county, and stands high in the estimation of the community.

BIOGRAPHY OF THE BRUMLEY FAMILY.

The Brumley family are old timers in the county, and no family stands higher than they. P. Brumley, George Brumley and Jim Brumley are worthy, noble men, are taxpayers and supporters of schools and churches, are debt-paying, God-serving men, are in easy circumstances and are perfectly reliable and trustworthy in all the relations of life, and can be depended upon to fulfill any obligation as promptly as any citizen of Hopkins County.

BIOGRAPHY OF ISAAC FANNING.

Isaac Fanning was born in the state of Alabama in the year 1832. The Fanning family came to Hopkins County in the year 1849. Isaac, the subject of this biographical sketch, was the second son of his father, Dr. Fanning, who was a prominent citizen and a useful man in the county in his day. Isaac came of a good, family, and inherited some of the noble traits of the character of his ancestors. In the year 1854 he married Mrs. Mary Tankersley; five children were born to this union, three of whom are living. They are all girls and are married. They are prolific women and are the mothers of thirty children. Mr. Fanning, after the loss of his companion, subsequently married Mrs. Elizabeth Johnson, daughter of Squire Means, a well-known citizen of Hopkins County in his day. Six children were born from this marriage—two boys and four girls. They are all respected citizens of the county. Mr. Fanning is living on his father's headright, within thirty yards of where his father built a log cabin in the year 1845. A part of this old homestead has been turned back to nature, and has grown into a dense forest, Mr. Fanning is seventy years of age. He works upon his farm, making a good hand at labor. He is a sober man of regular habits, and says, in referring to old times, that the flesh of bear is the sweetest and most wholesome meat he ever ate. In the year 1851 a man whose name Mr. Fanning has forgotten, and who was living with his family in Hopkins County, became tired of his married life and sought freedom from matrimonial bonds by murdering his companion, which he did by means of a bowie knife when she was altogether ignorant of his intentions. She was instantly killed by this cruel savage who claimed her as the wife of his bosom, without a moment's warning. The murderer well knew that the manhood of the Texan would resent this tragedy. He therefore arranged his affairs and left the county incognito. Sealin Stout was advised of this awful event and he and Mr. John Pitman were sent in pursuit of the fugutive. After several days and nights of close and hard riding they came upon the object of their search near where Grand Saline is now situated. It was during the heated weather, and they came upon him resting himself and horse in the shade of a beautiful grove of oak trees which stood invitingly by the wayside. No sooner had he discovered his suspected pursuers than he mounted his superb blooded animal and rode off hurriedly. They both called out imperatively for him to halt, which summons he positively refused to obey. No more commands were given nor quarters asked. The murderer was traveling in his shirt sleeves with his coat tied to the cantle of his saddle. One of the two pursuers said: "We will shoot him just where his suspenders cross upon his back." Sealin Stout raised his trusty fowling piece, took deliberate aim at the cross upon his back, and the unfortunate wretch fell from his animal dead in the road. Neither one of the men advanced a foot in the direction, of the dead man, but turned their own trusty animals in the direction of home and returned to their friends and reported the capture and death of the fugitive. Their friends received the news gladly, and gave the brave and courageous fellows a hearty greeting and a cordial welcome. This extraordinary event was told to Dr. Fanning by Sealin Stout, who spent a night with Dr. Fanning on his return from this trip. Isaac remembers quite distinctly hearing Mr. Stout repeat this incident.

BIOGRAPHY OF ED C. PETTY.

W. S. Petty, father of Ed Petty, was born in the state of North Carolina in the year 1804. He emigrated to the state of Texas in the year 1854. He married Mary Carlos in his native state. It is said that father Petty was the first man who conducted and controlled a railroad car in the United States. This car was propelled by horse power. As soon as the engine was supplanted by the use of steam he became the engineer, the first in the United States. W. S. Petty reared a family of five children—Robert E., James L., William Pitt, Martha E., Edward C., who is the subject of this sketch.   He now lives upon part of his father's old homestead. He married Miss Alice Wells of the state of Mississippi, when he was thirty years of age.   They have had eleven chil-

dren, nine of whom are living. They are all good
citizens of the county. There are four boys and
seven girls in this family. Mr. Petty has been
engaged in agricultural pursuits as a business of
life, and has had reasonable success as a planter.
He believes that the young should be educated and
has encouraged it in his family. His children
are bright, intelligent and are all well born. He
descended from a religious family and favors the
cause of Christianity; believing that preachers
should be paid for their services as well as other
professional men. His family are Methodists, and
give that church their support and encouragement. In politics he is a Democrat, and has no
patience with any of the isms that is not consistent
with Democracy. He is steadfast and firm in
his opinions, has been favored with the confidence
and esteem of his friends and acted in the capactiy
of county commissioner and gave entire satisfaction
to all his constituents. He has been a great hunter
and has always kept a large pack of trail dogs on
hand and enjoys a chase as well as any man. He
has been a successful marksman and has killed as
many as thirteen deer in the course of one day.
During a week's constant deer hunting he has
shot and killed as many as sixty head of deer.
His mother preserved the hams, which amounted
to one hundred and twenty in number. Mr. Petty
is equally fond of fishing and is said to be the most
successful angler in Hopkins County. Mr. Petty
gives an account of the migrating of the fox squir-

rels, which event took place in the year 1856. These squirrels came into the county from the direction of the northwest, in such large gangs as to attract attention and to alarm the citizens. This occurred in the fall of the year, and the planter was forced to stop everything he was engaged in in and begin at once to gather his corn crop. The squirrels were traveling east toward the great Mississippi River. The ladies who were engaged in washing for the families were forced, in order to rid their washing places of the squirrels, to use their battling sticks. Many of the pestiferous things were destroyed in this way. They were extremely fat—almost a burden to themselves. This strange phenomena was a great mystery to the populace at that time and is spoken of as one of the remarkable events of that day by the old-time settlers.

A CURIOUS INCIDENT.

George W. Johnson, an old and esteemed citizen of Hopkins County, a worthy planter and an all around fellow, enjoying the full confidence of his acquaintances, is living with his second wife. She was, at the time of her marriage to Mr. Johnson, the widow Hopper. He is the father of nine children, his wife is also the mother of nine children, and yet they have only thirteen in number. This appears to be a puzzle to the reader, but when figured aright the circumstance is real simple. The author leaves the reader free to solve the problem.

BIOGRAPHY OF A. T. MELSON.

A. T. Melson was born in the state of Georgia on the 4th of February, 1827, and grew to manhood in the home of his birth. His ancestors were old southern aristocracy, and a noble and manly set of gentlemen, while the women were unexcelled for purity and gentleness. At the age of twenty-two years Mr. Melson married Miss Martha Ransom, a daughter of Col. Samuel Ransom, a large slave holder and planter of great prominence in the county. Miss Martha was eighteen years of age when she married Mr. Melson. Within a few years after their marriage they moved to Hopkins County, Texas, where they have lived and raised their family. He settled upon the tract of land that he is now living upon forty-eight years ago. They have had born to them seven children. Four of this number are living and are well-known citizens of the county. There were three boys and one girl. W. C. married Miss Formby; she passed away and he subsequently married another Miss Formby, an own cousin of his first companion. He is a successful farmer and lives near his parents. Alex married Miss Wiley, and has for years been engaged in mercantile pursuits. He is living at this time in White Sulphur Springs, Indian Territory, his health having failed him in this county. J. M. Melson married Miss Fru Lanier, a daughter of William Lanier, a splendid gentleman and of good family. J. M. is an attorney at law and lives in Sulphur Springs, where he is engaged in the practice of his profession. He has been honored by his people to represent them in the legislature of his state, giving such satisfaction that he was returned for the third term; afterwards declining to offer himself for re-election. Miss Mary Melson, the only daughter, married William Tyser, a young man of fine business qualities and of good ancestors. Mr. Melson has experienced all the hardships of a pioneer life, is a sober, just and upright man, has always had the fullest confidence of his neighbors and acquaintances, being blessed with a companion of great force of character and indomitable will, with great energy and industry he has made life a fair success and is in independent circumstances. He and his wife are living alone at the old homestead, and are seemingly as happy as when they began the struggle for a respectable existence in the world.

BIOGRAPHY OF HARRISON ATTAWAY.

Harrison Attaway was born June 14th, 1848, in Henderson County, Tennessee. He came with his father into the state of Texas in the year 1855. He married Amanda Able in the year 1855. She was the daughter of Z. D. Able, an old-time citizen of Hopkins County, and one of its best men. His wife is a native of Texas, and is proud to be called a native Texan. They are the parents of sixteen children. There are thirteen of this number living. George F. is married and lives within half a mile

of where he was born. Elbert D., Mary, H. C.,
Jacob, Jonathan, Roger, W., Carroll, Paul, Elijah,
Martha M., Arminda, Bertha, Jena are all living
with their parents. They are as strong and as
healthy a set of children as can be found in Hopkins County. Seven of Mr. Attaway's children
are consistent members of the Christian church
at Como, which place is their father's home. In
an early day he was engaged in mercantile pursuits. Subsequently he turned his attention to
farming and to the raising of stock. He has by
industry and economy accumulated means sufficient to place him in easy and comfortable circumstances. He has ever set a good example before
his children. Not one of the large family uses
tobacco in any form, and have never been known
by their father to have bought one drop of in-
toxicating liquors, nor have they ever been in-
dicted by the courts for any kind of crime or mis-
demeanor. Mr. Attaway realizes the great benefit
accruing from a good, practical education, so he
is using every effort possible to educate his family
and thus prepare them for useful men and women.
He and his companion are members of the Baptist
church. While he is striving for a respectable
existence here on earth, he is not neglecting his
soul's salvation. He is a Prohibitionist, and he
practices what he preaches. He is a Mason in
good standing, and takes pride in visiting his
Lodge. Three of his sons are enthusiastic members of the Masonic fraternity. Mr. Attaway

has lived a useful life in Hopkins County. He
is happy in his surroundings, loves his neighbors
and his friends, fears God and expects to be rewarded in the great by-and-by.

BIOGRAPHY OF B. R. CARGILE.

B. R. Cargile was born in the state of Alabama
in the year 1851. He has lived in this county
since he left his native state. At the age of twenty-
one years he married Miss Georgie Thompson.
She died without offspring. He afterwards married Miss Alice Swafford of the state of Louisiana.
From this marriage eight children were born, only
four of whom are living. Tommie married Miss
Martha Bruton, a daughter of Reed Bruton, a
splendid citizen, a mechanic worthy of the name.
She was just sixteen years of age, a nice, beautiful
girl. Miss Corena is seventeen years of age; Miss
Ruthie, fifteen years; Miss Irma, thirteen years.
These good people are raising an orphan boy, and
are raising him as one of their own; he is treated just
as well in every particular. He is a farmer and
a cattleman and is making life successful. He
is rearing an interesting family, educating them
and preparing them for useful lives. He is a just,
law-abiding citizen and appreciates the laws of
his country that protect his life and property,
He supports the government by paying his taxes,
and does it without complaint. He has the full
confidence of everybody, is a well-known stockman

and a successful trader. His postoffice address is at Birthright, Hopkins County, Texas.

BIOGRAPHY OF HOWARD HARGRAVE.

Howard Hargrave was born in the state of Indiana in the year 1840. It was in the city of Booneville that he first saw the light of day. His parents migrated to the state of Texas in the year 1843. Howard was therefore three years of age. His father settled at old Sulphur Bluff with the rest of the Hargrave family. At this infantile age Howard remembers many incidents that took place under his observation—when the first mill was erected, the first blacksmith shop, the first wagon and wood shop, in fact was an eye witness to the upbuilding of old Sulphur Bluff, which place has long since passed into a howling wilderness. It was here at this Bluff that the first postoffice was established, the first store house owned and managed by Wash Cole, whose name has been mentioned in connection with this history, a grocery and drug cabin owned and run by John South. It was here that the first school house was built and the first school taught in Hopkins County. There were as many as one dozen families living here at one time. Robert Hargrave gave them employment, as he had several enterprises carried on at the old Bluff. The mail for this place was brought out from Paris, Lamar County, called at that time Pin Hook. The county was new—but few roads, no bridges, and there were times when

the Sulphur Creek was swollen to such an extent
that no mail could be had for weeks at a time.
For the want of mails the citizens at the Bluff were
in total ignorance as to what was going on in the
states.   The effect of any writing upon the public
mind is mathematically measured by its depth of
thought.   The way to speak and to write what
will ever be remembered is to speak and write
sincerely, honestly and truthfully.   At the age
of twenty-five years Howard married Miss Lida
Huskey, on July 13th, this day being selected on
account of its being the birthday of the groom.
Three children have been born to them: Eddie
married Miss Minnie Griffin.   He is engaged in
mercantile pursuits in Sulphur Bluff.   His business is a co-partnership one.   He has a couple of
interesting babies.   Miss Loma married Ed Murrie,
a firstrate fellow and a fine business gentleman
who merits the respect and confidence of his acquaintances,   They are the parents of two bright
children.   Mrs. Murrie is a bright, intelligent and
interesting lady, a star among her several friends
and is loved and esteemed for her noble qualities.
Guy Hargrave is the youngest child, a nice, gentle-
manly young fellow, who is chief clerk and manager at this time of the large business establishment
of Jacob M. Lindley, at Peerless, in Hopkins County.
He is a sober, honest and upright business man,
the pride of his aged parents, and the favorite of
his associates.   Howard is a man of great force of
character.   When his mind is fully made up on

any given point, he is firm and immovable. He
has been elected county commissioner, and served
his constituents well.   His voice was heard and
recognized in this body, always contending for
what he believed to be right, and was as open as
day in condemning the wrong.   He is not a member of any religious denomination, but encourages
the perpetuation of religious institutions by assisting in the substantial way.   This liberality has
been his religion; he having contributed more
money for this purpose than any citizen of his
neighborhood.   His heart has gone out with sympathy for the poor and needy.   No one has ever
been turned from his door in hunger and want.
It is said that at times he has given food and shelter
to as many as fifty needy persons at one time.
On one occasion when the winter storms were
raging, the earth freezing, the wind howling and
the drifting snow falling, he learned that a company of men, women and children were in camp
near his plantation without food or shelter.   He
immediately went to this camp and had the entire
company go to his residence and remain till the
storm subsided.   This he did without remuneration.   This is the act of a true philanthropist and
a man who makes no pretensions to Christianity.

BIOGRAPHY OF ALFRED J. HARGRAVE.

Uncle Jack, Alfred Hargrave, was born in the
state of Indiana in the year 1833 and came with
his parents to the territory of Hopkins County in

the year 1843 and located in the neighborhood of where he has lived all his life. There was only one cabin in the territory now Hopkins County when his father moved into it. This cabin was owned and occupied by one John Bivins, who soon disappeared from the territory and was never again heard from. It was supposed that some sad accident befell him and his family. There was a small log pen that was occupied by Billy and Harvey Hargrave, which my father moved into with them and remained until the fall of the year. My father afterwards moved some three miles north and built a double cabin out of rails split from the timber, and covered these pens with clapboards, which afforded us shelter through the coming winter, until a suitable cabin could be built. There was no convenience of any kind— we had to do any way to get along; but you see we did live through all these trials, hardships and disappointments. The people of to-day are ignorant of all these things that the pioneer must undergo. To tell of the many things—many of which were startling and alarming in their nature—would read like a fable. The country was overrun with wild beasts and wild animals of every kind that was common to this climate. Deer hams were preserved, dried and an abundant supply was always on hand. Bear meat, which was always fat and wholesome, was used to a great extent. There were very few hogs; but occasionally a hog or a sow and pigs could be seen around someone's cabin. The hog was afraid to go far into the range. The bear and the panther were the dog's greatest enemies. From instinct the hog dreaded these animals. Alfred Hargrave married Miss Harriett Barclay, a daughter of Hugh Barclay, an old pioneer citizen, at the youthful age of seventeen years, Nine children were born to them, six of whom are living. They all live near their father. They are all good citizens of Hopkins County. No family has a better record for fair, just and honest dealings than does this family. Alfred Hargrave has twenty-five grandchildren. Eighteen out of this number are boys—all healthy well born boys. He makes his home at this time with his son Glen, a kindly disposed man and an appreciative son, a kind and affectionate husband. On one occasion when Alfred's father had killed a large bear, the foot of the bear was thrown toward a sow. She took fright and ran away, forty miles distant.

BIOGRAPHY OF JAMES SPENCER.

J. M. Spencer was born in the state of Tennessee in the year 1833. At the age of twenty-five years he married Miss Tennessee Davis and immediately migrated to the state of Texas. He is the father of seven boys, all of whom are grown men and worthy citizens of Hopkins County—sober, moral, debt-paying, honest men, credit to themselves and an honor to their aged parents. Mr. Spencer lost his first companion by an unfortunate accident.

Her clothing caught on fire while she was engaged in soap making; she being alone at her home at the time of this gruesome and deplorable affair. She was an affectionate wife and a devoted mother. He subsequently married Mrs. Miranda McDougal, a woman blessed with a good share of common sense, a lady of refinement and taste. Mr. Spencer is a planter and stock-raiser, a man of sound judgment in all matters, a consistent member of the Christian church, and a splendid citizen of Hopkins County.

BIOGRAPHY OF T. L. SIMMS.

Jesse M. Simms, deceased, was born in the state of Georgia in the year 1813. At the age of twenty-two years he married Miss E. G. White in an adjacent county. In the year 1857 he moved with his family to Hopkins County, Texas. They were the parents of three children—two girls and one boy. The eldest, Miss Martha, married John P. Orr, a distant relative, and raised a large and respectable family in Hopkins County. The youngest, Miss Penelope, married Rev. James Christian, a Baptist preacher and a splendid gentleman. T. L. Simms married Miss Minter at the age of twenty-four years, She was a daughter of Uncle Joe Minter, an old Texan whom all loved for his many noble qualities of heart and soul. By this marriage twelve children were born, nine of whom are living. Mr. Simms' family are all about grown.

There are two living at home with their parents. They are all worthy of mention in this history— sober, industrious honest, just and truthful. He has used great care and caution in training and educating his children, and with the help of a noble wife and mother to assist, advise, counsel and admonish, he has been successful in rearing first-class children. He has followed farming and raising a few cattle, all through life. He is in comfortable circumstances; always ready and willing to meet all legal and lawful demands. His house is well furnished and his table well supplied, and his friends are at all times welcome and encouraged. He has been a Democrat in politics, and has been honored by his party to fill important positions in the county, the duty of which he has discharged to the satisfaction of his constituents. He has ever been honest, sincere and absoluiely conscientious in all of his relations with his fellow men, in private life as well as in public life. He is a consistent member of the Bapitst church, and his membership is at old Bethel Church. Askew is his postoffice address, a new office, recently established, the name of which is given in honor of the Askew family, a family famous for its many good and noble traits of character. Mr. Simms believes the young should be educated, thereby better qualifying them to become better and more useful citizens. He was an old soldier in the Confederate army, and volunteered to serve his country while in college, leaving one of the best schools in that day in all of the country. He was promoted and acted as Sergeant Major in the Thirty-second Texas Regiment, Ector's Brigade. He succeeded Luther Williams, father of Jno. D. Williams, of Sulphur Springs. Luther Williams was killed at Richmond, Kentucky. He was as brave and courageous a soldier as ever wore the gray. Mr. Simms is sixty-one years old, has spent his life in Hopkins County. His father possessed the only cotton gin for miles around. It was propelled by horse power, manufacturing a couple of bales of cotton per day. The seed from which the lint had been taken would accumulate, to his disturbance, in such large quantities that his father absolutely refused to gin cotton unless the owner pledged himself to remove his seed from the gin-house. He offered inducements to any one that would haul his seed from the gin. How different are the conditions that confront the citizens that raise cotton in this day! Cotton seed is now in great demand at twenty dollars per ton, each owner of a bale of cotton demanding every seed. The author lived in the same section of the county that Mr. Simms is living in at this time, forty-five years ago. At that time water was quite scarce and difficult to obtain Now springs are to be seen, and wells may be had at a reasonable distance below the surface of the earth. We leave this strange phenomenon to the geologists to settle and determine the cause of the wonderful change in nature.

BIOGRAPHY OF THE CHAPMAN FAMILY.

J. Elias Chapman was born in the state of Indiana, July 15th, 1848, and came to Texas with his parents in the year 1851. His grandfather was born in the year 1793. He migrated from South Carolina to the state of Indiana and from there moved into the state of Texas in the year 1850. Elias' grandmother was born in the year 1796. Her maiden name was Polly Gray. These old people were united in marriage in the year 1816. Elias' grandfather was a Methodist preacher and lived for a while and preached in the state of Kentucky, where Elias' father was born in the year 1818. His father married Mary E. Smith in the state of Indiana in the year 1845. Three children were born to them in that state. Their names are W. R., J. E., and J. S. Chapman. His parents then moved to the state of Texas and settled where he lived until death in what is known as Chapman Arm. George, the nominee for county commissioner, an honest and justly popular citizen; Shed, who has served his county as tax collector on several occasions; and Doctor, a successful physician and a useful man; Ellen and Eva —all were born in Hopkins County. W. R. and Ellen are dead. This entire family are citizens of Hopkins County. Elias' father has one brother, Willis, and a sister, Polly Ann, who married J. V. Logsdon in the year 1855. The father of Elias was named James and was known as Uncle Jimmie Chapman. He was a man whose heart was as big as all out-of-doors.

Elias married Miss Ida Cobb in the year 1881.
She was a step-daughter of Billie Moore. They
have eight children, who are all bright, intellectual,
healthy and well born. He has taught his children
industrious habits. His boys are natural mechan-
ics, can construct any article out of wood or iron
that they choose. John S. married Mattie Harper,
the daughter of G. W. Harper, better known as
Wash, an old Texan, a just, upright and honest
man of remarkable energy and enterprise. They
have five children, whom he is striving to educate
and to make good citizens. He is rearing his family
upon a farm, and teaching them to work as well as
educating them in books. George W. married
Dosca France in the year 1890. They have only
two children: Melson, a son; and Pearl, a daughter.
Shed married Miss Jessie Harris in the year 1897.
They have no issue. Dr. Chapman married Miss
Dama McCullock. They have one child, an infant.
They were married in the year 1899. Ellen married Marion Harris in the year 1886, and has two
children. Eva married Thos. Searls, a clean, nice
gentleman, in the year 1883. They have six
children. Mr. Searls is a well to do farmer, owns
his own plantation, and is making life a success.
His children are all stout, well-formed, bright,
interesting children, of good habits. This large
family of Chapmans are remarkable for their plain
common sense, their sobriety, honesty, industry
and general usefulness in many particulars. They
are all making money and doing well. They

are big-hearted people, are not little or parsimoni-
ous or picaunish in their transactions; but are
free-hearted, liberal, generous and as open as day.
No family in Hopkins County enjoys a better
reputation or has a wider circle of friends, or is
more generally known than the Chapman family.
By industry they have accumulated sufficient of
this world's goods to place them in easy and comfortable circumstances, and it affords them great
satisfaction and pleasure to extend their generosity
and unselfish hospitality to their friends. Their
motto is to keep up a smiling countenance, an
open heart and a good exertion. They all have
order and much system in their management of
affairs, and are mild and pleasant in their families;
but their rules of discipline must be observed and
obeyed.

BIOGRAPHY OF WILLIS CHAPMAN.

William Chapman, father of Benjamin, James,
Willis and Ellis Chapman, came to Hopkins County
in the year 1850. Willis, his son, coming in ad-
vance of his father about one year. William Chapman, father of Willis, lived in the county until
the year 1872, and passed away, and is buried in
Hopkins County, at the family burying ground.
His four sons lived as citizens of Hopkins county
until they were removed by death. Willis is the
only surviving son. He married Nancy Bottoms
in the year 1855. Five children were born to

them. Three of this number are living: J. E. and
J. W. Chapman and Mrs. M. M. Davis. Willis
had the great misfortune to lose his companion
in the year 1869. Subsequently he married Miss
Harriet Smith, daughter of a prominent physician
of Hopkins County. By this marriage eight children were born to them, five of whom are living.
When Willis came into Hopkins County, the county
site had just been located at Tarrant. There
were some ten or twelve buildings, including court-
house and jail, which was constructed of small
logs, and there were only a few permanent settlers
in the county. Dr. O. S. Davis, who is well known
all over Hopkins County, moved to where Sulphur
Springs is now situated, and began to advertise
the medicinal properties of the sulphur water in
such favorable terms that people came from all
directions and camped around the spring in tents,
during the summer season, and used the water
for their health. The change of water proved
beneficial, and within a short period of time people
began to buy lands and settle in the vicinity of the
springs. Soon a class of very worthy and desira-
ble citizens began to move into the advertised
section. This incident is, perhaps, why Dr. Davis
is called the father of Sulphur Springs. Mr.
Chapman is living to-day upon the same tract
of land that he first settled upon when he began
to fight the battles of life. He has always been
happy and contented with his condition in life. He
is kindly disposed, good natured, a member of

the Methodist church, and a worker for the cause
of Christ, has faith in his God and feels that he
will be rewarded in the end.

BIOGRAPHY OF RED COLLINS.

Red Collins, one of the oldest timers in the
county, was born in the state of Missouri in the
year 1833. He came to Texas with his father in
the year 1839 and stopped in Red River district
near where Clarksville is now located. The whole
country was a perfect wilderness, even what few
people were here were hardly civilized. In that
day the most of the male inhabitants were refugees
from justice, having committed some crime against
the laws of the state from which they emigrated.
Not being of a first-class people, and coming into
the wilds of a new country, their actions and deeds
knew no restraint and many times their conduct
was a source of annoyance and often a terror to
the law-abiding element among the few citizens
who had moved into the county, many of whom
left the Republic and returned to the state from
which they had come. In the year 1840 many
emigrants came into Texas and received a hearty
welcome from the early settlers. "Misery loves
company." This gang of ruffians soon gave place
to a better class of people and the country soon wore
an aspect of civilization. Mr. Collins has seen
men shot down at the gambling tables and at mustang pony races, in as reckless a manner as if they

were nothing more than wild beasts. There was no law to restrain the murderer, none to restrain the thief, save that of mob law, which was frequently resorted to for the protection of the better element of citizens. In the year 1844 the citizens of Hopkins County pursued and arrested four men of this murderous gang, and after a kind of court-marshal or mock trial, the entire number were hung. This hanging was done some four miles northwest from Black Jack Grove on Smith's prairie, near Dunbar branch. People came a distance of one hundred miles to see this gang of thieves executed, and to engage in the execution. A desperado whose name was Johnson, originally from the state of Missouri, was the leader of this gang of outlaws. Rev. Wash Barker, Capt. Merrit Branom and Dave Hopkins were at this execution and rendered service on the occasion by guarding the prisoners and encouraging the hanging. Mr. Collins, at the age of twenty-four years married Miss Malinda Fanning, daughter of Dr. Fanning an old pioneer physician and a worthy gentleman. Four children were born to this union. One of these children is dead, the others are married, have families and are doing well. All have useful husbands, who are good citizens of the county. Mr. Collins had the misfortune to lose his wife, and subsequently married Miss Virginia Scarborough. By this marriage nine children came to them. Four of this number are married and are respected citizens of the county; the remaining five live at home with their parents, and bid fair to make good and useful citizens of the county. Mr. Collins has been successful, and has given all of his children a good home. He has wisely made provision for the homes of the younger members of his family who are under his control and protection. He has no patience with evil doing, and has never been known, even among the wilds of early life, to encourage a dishonest deed. Red Collins, Red Crisp and Samps Crisp, a negro boy, gave the names of the following creeks in Hopkins County: Coffey Creek, Dry Creek, Running Creek, and Elm Creek. Mr. Collins is now in feeble health.

BIOGRAPHY OF THE MINTER FAMILY.

Joseph T. Minter, deceased, was born in Putnam County, Georgia, in the year 1818. He married Miss Sarah A. Carter, in the same state, at the age of seventeen years. She was a daughter of a prominent planter and slave holder. In the year 1853 Mr. Minter migrated to Hopkins County, Texas, and lived in the county until he died. They were the parents of twelve children, nine of whom are living; and all are citizens of the county. Ann E. married W. D. Byrd and raised a large family of boys and girls who are citizens of the county. William H. married Sarah Smith, a daughter of a farmer, a good man and a good citizen. He married in the year 1863. Morgan Minter married

Ada Askew, daughter of Capt. R. L. Askew, a prominent citizen of Hopkins County. Morgan has raised an unusually large family. They were married in the year 1864. Miss Fannie Minter married Thomas L. Simms, a gentleman of good family and most excellent parentage. They married in the year 1864, and have raised a large and useful family in the county. Miss Dollie married John Stephens, a Georgia gentleman, a man of good business qualifications and of good character. They were married in the year 1867, and have no offspring. Robert A. married Susan Rainey, a splendid lady of excellent birth. They have a large family of intelligent children with industrious habits. Sylvanus has been twice married. He is one of the best men in Hopkins County. To know him is to love him. He is a big-hearted nobleman, meriting all the respect and esteem he enjoys. He is a widower at this time. Mattie E., a most excellent lady, loved for her many good qualities, married John Denney, an all around splendid fellow. They were the parents of four children. Mr. Denney died, and subsequently Mrs. Denney married M. O. Minter, a relative. He is a kindly disposed, good-natured-gentleman, of splendid business qualifications. Gus Minter, the youngest child of this large family, married Miss Sallie Renow. She died and he afterwards married Rebecca Atkins, an Old State lady of good birth. He is engaged in mercantile pursuits, and does business at the place where he was born.

This family are all good citizens of Hopkins County.
The boys are highly esteemed, are honest, just, debt-
paying men, and have the full confidence of all
with whom they deal. The girls all married good
men, and are in happy conditions. They are all
taxpayers in the county; are church members;
liberal, enterprising, useful and industrious men.
They are good to the poor and needy—never re-
fusing the deserving of their assistance. They all
occupy a leading place in society, and are very
highly respected by everybody—a quiet, good,
moral set of men, that Hopkins County should
be proud to acknowledge as citizens.

BIOGRAPHY OF R. R. WILLIAMS.

R. R. Williams emigrated from the state of
Arkansas in the year 1866 and located in Black
Jack Grove, where he has since lived. He married Miss Susan Ward at the age of twenty-two
years, in Arkansas. Nine children were the result of
this union, six of whom are living. They are all
citizens of the county, live near their parents and are
doing well. Mr. Williams descended from a long
line of ancestors. He can trace his family name
back to Roger Williams, he has taken an active
part in the politics of his county, espousing the
cause of Democracy, and has ever been steadfast
in the faith. He has served his country as a soldier,
and was faithful in the discharge of his duty.
He commanded a company of cavalry scouts in

front of Gen. Price's army. In the year 1864 he was captured by the northern troops, was condemned to be shot for guerrilla fighting, but later he proved that he was a Confederate soldier, and was consigned to prison. He took a prominent part in the reconstruction of Texas. He has lived for thirty-four years in Hopkins County, and during that time he has filled many honorable positions. In the year 1900 he was elected a member of the 27th Legislature of Texas, giving satisfaction to his constituents.

BIOGRAPHY OF L. A. LOLLAR, DECEASED.

L. A. Lollar was born in the state of Tennessee in the year 1829, and came to Hopkins County in the year 1849. He married Miss Mary Veal in the year 1854, who still survives him. They had eight children born to them: seven sons and one daughter; five of whom are living. John, the eldest son has been twice married and is living in the county with his second wife. Miss Lula married Sam Matthews, a common-sense business man of good judgment. He is a just and honest man. Buster married Miss Lula Sparks, daughter of John Sparks, a prominent stock man. Bird married Miss Dora Bennett, a sister of Ben Bennett and a granddaughter of Uncle Bob Cannon. Levi married Mada Turner, daughter of Squire Turner. The sons of L. A. Lollar are all industrious, reliable men. They are all taxpayer of the county, and are numbered

among the best citizens of the county. Mr. Lollar
established himself in the mercantile business in
the year 1855, which he prosecuted with great energy
and success up to his death. Although he met
with many serious reverses and losses. He
never made any public profession of religion, nor
did he ever attach himself to any denomination,
or to any secret order or society, yet he was a man
of great benevolence, generous, kind, upright, just
and truthful in all the relations of life. No man
was ever turned from his door in hunger and want.
He was a man of feeble constitution and suffered
greatly in his last illness and seemed to realize
that his time on earth was short. A few hours
before his demise he sent for Judge Rogers of
Sulphur Springs a friend in whom he had unbounded confidence and had him to write his will which
was done. He then placed his business in the care
of Judge Rogers with that same business capacity
that was characteristic of his life. After that he
called each one of his family by name and gave to
each one special counsel, and his last wishes. During
his long residence in this county and his extensive
dealings with the public no one has ever charged
him with deplicity or with a dishonest act. Mr.
Lollar was an old pioneer citizen and experienced
many hardships in an early day in Texas. He
was among the first to open the way to civilization.
His sons all seem to have the same business foresight of their departed father.

BIOGRAPHY OF JESSE C. GARRETT.

J. C. Garrett was born in the State of Tennessee in the year 1840, and moved to Hopkins County, in the year 1863 with his father Presly Garrett. With the exception of a few years he has lived in the county continuously since. At the age of twenty five he married Miss E. J. Garrett a distant relative. By this marriage eleven children were born to them, five boys and six girls, eight of whom are living at the present time. W. E. married Miss Willie McFall, he is a farmer, a taxpayer and a good citizen of the county. John P. married Miss Tempie Lenon, he is an all around business fellow. Martha A. married J. D. Blount, a farmer of industrious habits. C. C. married D. T. Knowls. Melissa married Frank Pippin. Emma Lou married T. P. Lee, a farmer. Miss S. C. is single and lives with her parents. The youngest whose name is Lawrence Sullivan Ross and lives at home. This family is a remarkable one in some respects. They are sober, moral, industrious, honest upright men, and all merit the respect and esteem of the entire county. They are social, genial and hospitable, and are a good class of people to meet. The mother of these children was raised in Texas, being here in an early day she has experienced the trials and hardships common to pioneer life. She has been an eye witness to many gangs of wild Indians as they would pass her father's home. She has seen many buffaloes, and saw her father shoot and kill one within one hundred yards of his house. She is a hail, hearty, healthy woman, and physicially able to perform all of her household duties to the entire satisfaction of all concerned. Mr. Garrett has engaged in Indian fighting and assisted in driving the Indians from the country. He was a soldier during the Civil war, was elected Captain of a company and served during the war as such. He was faithful in the discharge of his duties as an officer, and held the respect and confidence of his men to the end. He and his wife are both members of the Primitive Baptist Church. He has never turned any one from his door hungry and in want. He is in easy circumstances. He is loved for his noble qualities of mind and heart.

BIOGRAPHY OF J. A. WEAVER, DECEASED.

The Col. J. A. Weaver family was a prominent family in Hopkins County, there are only two of this noted family living in the county at this time. W. B. Weaver who married Celia Patrick, a daughter of a prominent and successful merchant of Sulphur Springs. Miss Sallie married Phil Foscue, cashier of the First National Bank of Sulphur Springs, and as noble hearted gentleman as we have in the county, true to his convictions and solid in his business matters.

Col. Weaver was foremost in many public enterprises in the county; was high sheriff and tax collector for eight years. He was a leading member of the Methodist church; noted for his liberal donations, for his charity, and was an influential man in state and county affairs until his death. His widow, a most estimable lady, survives him. Wm. Weaver, brother to J. A. Weaver, left only one child, a daughter, Miss Dora, who married Allie McKenzie. He is a progressive farmer and stock raiser, and is making life a success, a splendid citizen and a heavy tax payer in the county.

BIOGRAPHY OF THE LANDERS FAMILY.

This family are well and favorably known all over the county. They are among the first settlers of the county. Landers creek, in the county, is named in honor of this old pioneer family. Andy Landers, George, John and Dick Landers are old men now, they were raised in the county and form a part of the history of the county. They are good moral men, worthy of the respect and confidence of the community—all have nice, respectable, industrious families and are doing well. They are property owners and are progressive in their views and have contributed in no small degree to the material development and prosperity of the city and of the county. They and their companions are consistent members of the Christian church.

BIOGRAPHY OF CRAWFORD MAYES.

Crawford S. Mayes was born in Burkes County, Georgia, in the year 1840. He came into Texas in the year 1866, and married Miss Mary E. Hooser of Red River County in the year 1873, and moved into Hopkins County and settled where he is still living. They are the parents of eight children equally divided as to sex. Mr. Mayes is a successful farmer and an all around business man. He was a soldier in the time of the war, is a quiet citizen in time of peace, is a devoted husband, a kind and loving father, a good neighbor and a splendid citizen. He was made a prisoner during the Civil war, and spent several months in the walls of a northern prison. No man under the sun ever existed that is more liberal or more generous to those in whom he confides. His home is a home of hospitality, and the citizens have learned this fact; which is evidenced by the large amount of company he has on all public occasions. He is a law-abiding man, a church supporter, and a debt-paying gentleman.

BIOGRAPHY OF CROCKETT CAMPBELL.

Crockett H. Campbell was born in 1816, and is eighty-six years of age. He came to Hopkins County in the year 1841. There was not a single cabin on the south side of North Sulphur Creek at that time. Buffalo herds were roaming all over the country. He has shot and killed a number of buffalo as well as all kinds of animals and wild beasts. Indians were to be seen and heard in many places, and a few people who were living in tents were in constant and perpetual dread of them. Many emigrants who came into the new country, became dissatisfied, alarmed, and returned to their old homes in the States. In the year 1843 he married Elizabeth Collins. By this union eight children were born, four of whom are living. He had the misfortune to lose his wife, and subsequently married Miss Mary Couch. They were the parents of eight children, six boys and two girls. Four of these children are dead, the others live near their parents, and are good, worthy citizens of Hopkins County. Crockett has farmed and raised stock all of his life. He is a man of noble qualities. His example has been good. He is beloved by all who know him. He is old now, and suffering from the weakness of age ; therefore his memory is impaired and his body is feeble. Since this writing he has passed away.

BIOGRAPHY OF JAMES A. SIMMS.

James A. Simms, deceased, was born in the state of Georgia. When he arrived at his majority he married Miss Emily Jane Hansom, a daughter of a prominent slave holder and planter in the same neighborhood in which he was raised. He moved into Hopkins County in the year 1853, where he settled and raised a large and interesting family. Jonathan Simms, was his eldest child. The others were Uca C., Tom K., Amanda, J. M. Simms, Jr., Britton B., Bianca, and Kendrick D., three of these children are living in the county. Uca C. is now Mrs. Shugart, a prosperous farmer and a worthy citizen, of noble qualities. J. M., Jr. is a doctor of high standing, and is appreciated for his skill as a physician and as a citizen of noble and generous impulses. He married Miss Annie L. Lacy, a Hopkins County lady of excellent family and good blood. Brooks Simms married Miss Robertson, daughter of Thomas Robertson, a Baptist preacher. The name of the Simms family is prominent in the county. Some of the best citizens in the county are among them. They are all sober, high-minded gentlemen, and well worthy of the good name they bear.

BIOGRAPHY OF DR. HOUSTON.

The C. M. Houston family is an old pioneer family, only three of this large family are living in the county at this time: Columbus, Julia and Mary. They are all married and are doing well, and are good citizens of Hopkins County. Miss Julia married Mark Fuqua; Miss Mary married John Longino.

BIOGRAPHY OF W. S. WHITE, DECEASED.

W. S. White raised a large family in the county. He was justice of the peace for a greater length of time than any man who ever lived in the county. He served in that capacity for twenty-five years. His family form a part of the history of the county. His sons are all farmers and well-to-do citizens,

respected and appreciated for their industry and
energy. All are taxpayers and good citizens.
His daughters married men who are hard-working,
honest, good citizens of the county, and who are
highly esteemed as such. They are all advocates
of education and church enterprises.

BIOGRAPHY OF J. C. STOUT.

My father, Sealin Stout, was born in the state
of Arkansas in the year 1818. He died in Hopkins
County at the age of seventy-eight. No life in
Hopkins County was more eventful or attended
with more romance than was that of Sealin Stout.
He has often been referred to as being prominent
in many exciting incidents in this history. Sealin's
father crossed Red River on a raft built with his
own hands, when Sealin was only one month old,
and settled in Red River District, where Sealin
grew to manhood amid the wilds of the country.
In the year 1836 he was engaged in Indian fighting;
afterwards he fought for Texas Independence, and
was a soldier in the Mexican war. After peace
was concluded he came home and married Elvira
Richey. By this union eleven children were born:
nine boys and two girls. John, the oldest son,
lives in Bowie County. Frank lives in Hopkins
county, and married a daughter of old Dr. Payne,
a pioneer citizen. Marion and Andrew both live
in Red River County, and are good, substantial
citizens. J. C. Stout married Miss Mary Brook-

shire, a daughter of Jesse Brookshire, an old-time citizen and a man of good character. N. S. Stout married Miss Laura Miller, a daughter of Dr. Christian. Miss Martha Stout married Ed Henley. They are the parents of Elizabeth Henley, who married Dr. Buck Sparks, a young physician. Elizabeth inherited some of the noble traits of character of her grandfather, Sealin Stout. Bill Stout married a sister of Mrs. J. C. Stout. He is dead. Robert married Miss Georgia Crain, a niece of Ben Shepperd, a noble Christian gentleman. S. S. married Mattie Miller. Miss Mollie married Jim Pogue, a son of Thos. Pogue, who is a gentleman by inheritance. No cleaner people live in Hopkins County than the Pogue family.

BIOGRAPHY OF G. M. CALVERT.

G. M. Calvert was raised in Williamson County, Illinois. He came to the state of Texas when he was a young man, in the year 1854. Finally, after traveling almost across the American Continent, he returned to Illinois and married Miss Sophia Woodul in the year 1857. At the time of his marriage he was engaged in mercantile pursuits. Subsequently he sold his interests to other parties and migrated to Texas, and has, for a number of years, been a citizen of Hopkins County. He is well known as a practical-minded man, having introduced several important industries in the county. He believes in man's capability, and is a substantial advocate of all undertakings for the betterment of his county. He has been twice married, and has given his children every advantage possible, to assist them in becoming good and useful citizens. He is possessed of an ambitious spirit, has pride of character, and is careful in maintaining a good name. His example is good. Although an Agnostic, no man is more liberal, more generous or more hospitable than George M. Calvert. He is independent in thought, as open as day, and as honest and just as it is possible for mortal man to be. He enjoys the full confidence, respect and esteem, not only of the rank and file, but of the clergy as well.

BIOGRAPHY OF H. H. NANCE.

H. H. Nance was born in the state of Tennessee in the year 1838. He came to Hopkins County with his parents in the year 1857. Two years later he married Miss Susan Wells, a daughter of a Methodist preacher from the state of Georgia. From this union six children were born. Charles E. is a farmer and a good citizen of the county. He married Miss McGinnis. Elizabeth married J. K. Lewis. Joseph R. married Miss Lulu Bevis, an Alabama girl of good family. Miss Tealy married C. A. Bland and lives in Fannin County. Chester married Nora Harrison. Olga married Miss Roxey. Mr. Nance's family are all good citizens of the county, are doing well, and are respected. They are honest and upright in their dealings. He suffered a great loss in the death of the mother of these children. He, however, married Mrs. P. H. Richey, a splendid lady, with whom he is spending his life pleasantly. They have two children living: Allen B. and Annie Bertha. They are living with their parents at home. He has given his attention to farming and raising stock, and is in easy circumstances, able to meet with promptness all his liabilities. He is a taxpayer in the county, and believes in upholding and supporting the government that protects his life and property. He is a member of the Methodist church—has lived a devoted Christian for forty years. He helps the churches in a substantial way. Besides feeding many visitors to his church yearly, his doors are always open to the meritorious and the worthy. He comes from a good family, of Irish extraction, and advocates liberality in all things. His example has been good all through life—sober, honest, just and upright. He always has plenty to divide with his less fortunate neighbor, and manifests a disposition of generosity in all of his donations to churches and other needed enterprises.

BIOGRAPHY OF COGHAN RANSOM.

Croghan M. Ransom was born in the state of Georgia in the year 1833. In the year 1855 he married Miss Susan Hanson in Heard County,

Georgia; and immediately he and his bride left the state of Georgia and came to Texas and stopped in Hopkins County, where Mr. Ransom still lives. Twelve children were born to this marriage, six of whom are living. John, the eldest son, married Miss Looney Titsworth, and lives in San Saba County. Martillus married John Tom Jennings. They live in Chickasha, Indian Territory. They have no children—are prosperous and well-to-do. Robert S. married Miss Della Kirby. They live in the county and have no living children. Miss Mank married Frank Waller. They have five children, are citizens of the county, and are doing well. Dick married Miss Lula Baker, daughter of Bill Baker. They have one child and live at Winsboro, in Wood County. Miss Lou married W. L. Scruggs, a farmer, and lives in the county. Mr. Ransom has engaged in agricultural pursuits and followed farming all his life. He is highly respected, so is his family. He suffered a great calamity in the loss of his wife—the mother of his children—in the year 1879. He subsequently married Mrs. Mary Holdridge, with whom he is living at the present time. They have no children. Mr. Ransom has inherited good blood. His ancestors were prominent slave holders and wealthy people; stood high in money circles, and were a leading element in the state of Georgia.

A SUICIDE.

Not many years since, a young man made his will and then committed suicide. Here is his will in substance:

"I leave to society a ruined character. I leave to my father and mother as much misery as, in their feeble state they can bear. I leave to my brother and sisters the memory of my misspent life. I leave to my wife a broken heart, and to my children the memory that their father filled a drunkard's grave, and has gone to a drunkard's hell."

This is a sermon written on a coffin and it ought to reach a good many men who are fools, and who know they are fools, and who would rather drift than pull up. It is a good idea once in a while for a man to interview himself and ask: "What kind of a legacy am I leaving to my wife and children." That does not refer to money alone, in these days of business prudence every man tries to arrange his affairs so that when he passes away the burdens he leaves behind will rest lightly on his loved ones. There are morals, a man owes to his children's health, and if he is a drunkard how can he, according to nature's law, hope for robust offspring. He wants his children to live in an atmosphere of respectability and peace and decency. If he makes his life one long debauch, is he strong enough to drop his burden of immorality and sin at the door as he enters his home and appear to be a gentleman in the presence of his family. So many men refuse to think. They are selfish in their thoughts. Every man has some influence, no man can live wholly in himself. He leaves a legacy for some one. It may be a memory of kind words, of tender love and thoughtful devotion. It may be sorrow and shame, children with twisted limbs and unhealthy bodies, a woman with misery written in her eyes, parents who weep when a name is mentioned. Pity the man who has blasted the life that God gave him that the world is glad when six feet of earth hides his coffin, and hides him from the sight of mortal man. Man can live in a gluttonous manner with his desires for gain and greed unappeased until cultivated to that extent that he will sacrifice every enjoyment, every particle of human feeling to gratify his greed and at last prove himself nothing more than a hog. It has been said that all misers are nothing more, nothing less than hogs, and are unfit for the associations of the noble in heart, the generous in spirit, and are of no possible benefit to society until after they are dead and buried.—Such is the case with the hoggish man who has never cherished one thought outside of himself. Ah, my dear fellow, the world has no use for you until you are dead, and when you are gone people will rejoice. No kindly act of yours will ever be referred to, you will simply die and that is all of it.

BIOGRAPHY OF THE CLIFTONS.

The Clifton name is prominent in Hopkins County. Frank and John Clifton are pioneer citizens of Hopkins County. Uncle Frank is a primitive Baptist preacher, and is as straight and honest a man as the God of heaven desires man to be; his word is his bond, it is law and the people of the county understand it just that way. A pure, noble-hearted, God-serving gentleman, possessed of as few faults as any living man. John Clifton lives near Miller Grove and is a splendid citizen of Hopkins County. He has lived an upright, just and honest life, and has ever been loved and respected for his manly qualities, and generous disposition, and unusual hospitality extended to friends at his home. He is in feeble health now, is old and is living a very retired life.

BIOGRAPHY OF JACK STURDIVANT, DECEASED.

Jack Sturdivant was an old time Texan. He married in an early day in Tennessee and came to Hopkins County, Texas, where he has raised a family of children that are all grown up citizens now. Two of his offsprings are living in the county. David, who lives in Peerless, is one of his sons, a solid representative citizen who enjoys the confidence and respect of all who know him. He has twice been married. Miss Susie married De Tennison, a business man who appreciates his wife, loves his family and friends; honest and just and faithful in friendship, and a number one citizen— a heavy taxpayer. Uncle Jack's wife, Aunt Becca, still survives him. She owns an estate which she rents and lives handsomely upon the proceeds and is in independent circumstances. She is an agreeable kind hearted woman whom all respect.

BIOGRAPHY OF HENRY RUSSELL.

Uncle Henry Russell is one of the old land marks of the county, having lived in the county since its organization. He has been considered among the best and most substantial men in the county. He has always been an honest, upright, just man, and is appreciated for these qualities. His family are all highly respected and are a leading class in the county. He has three children: Joe Russell, a splendid man and a worthy citizen. Joe has a nice family and all are very much esteemed. John Russell is another son who has a most excellent lady for a wife; they are popular in society and highly respected by all who know them. Uncle Henry's daughter married John Odom, an exemplary man of noble qualities and generous disposition and has the confidence and love of his acquaintance, and is regarded by all as a first class citizen. The Russell name is familiar to all of the early settlers of Hopkins County.

BIOGRAPHY OF BLACKWELL FAMILY.

This noted family has long lived in Hopkins County, being amongst its first settlers. J. P.

Blackwell, deceased, raised a fair sized family of intelligent, worthy children, they are all citizens of Delta County. J. P. Blackwell was a useful man in his community, and was highly esteemed, he married Miss Rattan, a sister of Volney Rattan, one of the most conscientious, brave and courageous men which is in the knowledge of the writer; true to any cause he advocates as the needle is to the pole. Dr. Joel Blackwell is a son of J. P. Blackwell, a practicing physician and one of the leading doctors of the county of Delta. Page Blackwell is a brother of J. P., a splendid man, and a good reliable citizen. Erastus Blackwell is well known all over North East Texas as being a gentleman of exceptional good habits, kindly disposed, liberal and generous, a devoted husband, an affectionate father, a heavy taxpayer, and a just and upright gentleman, respected and beloved by all. He is one of the most elegant men, and sincere friend the writer ever knew, and when he passes away people will mourn for him from palace to hut. There are many good citizens now living in Delta County that aided years ago in making Hopkins County the prosperous county it is to-day. Squire John Boyd now deceased raised a large family of lovable girls, who have all married men of honor, worth and integrity. The name of Shuffield is well remembered by the old timers as being first class people in every particular. The family of Pickens are well and favorably known as old time Texas people, they are a good class of citizens and are highly respected as such.   Robert Hooten is an old timer, and lives in Delta County, he is a pure good man, honest and noble, with a heart full of charity.   Liberal in his views, and a Christian by name and nature.   He is a brother to Billie Hooten, one of Hopkins County's best citizens.

BIOGRAPHY OF THE KING FAMILY.

L. D. King married Miss Mary E. Hopkins, a daughter of Eldridge Hopkins.   They have reared a family of interesting children—four boys and three girls.   They are all married and have homes of their own.   Sam, their oldest son, was born in the year 1859, in old Tarrant.   B. F. King was born the 8th day of July, 1863.   The next in order of birth died after living twelve months.   Bob Lee King was born in 1868,   She married John Cummings.   W. E. was born in 1870.   Miss Kate married Ham Sickles, the son of Uncle Bill Sickles, an old pioneer citizen whom everybody loved and respected.   Miss Maud King married H. C. Connor. Capt. L. D. King is a lawyer, and has ever enjoyed a large practice.   He is thoroughly posted in all the theories of legal practice, and has an extensive knowledge of the decisions of the courts, both State and Federal.   He is aged now.   His life has been useful to Hopkins County, and honorable to himself, his friends and his family.   Prof. Sam King is a school teacher of marked ability, and has great aptitude for the profession, being a born teacher and a gentleman of honor and integrity. Prof. King has distinguished himself as a teacher of literature in Hopkins County. H. C. Connor is a lawyer and is at this time serving as District Judge by the will of the voters of his district. He is prompt and self-possessed, is thoroughly conversant with the rules of practice in the courts, and has an inexhaustible fountain of legal lore from which to draw at any moment. He is an honorable, high-minded gentleman, and an impartial judge. He was born and raised in Hopkins County.

THE COUNTY OFFICIALS.

The following named persons compose the county officials:

R. B. Keasler,	County Judge
D. Thornton,	County Attorney
W. B. Loving,	Sheriff
John Moreland,	Treasurer
W. H. Dickerson,	Tax Collector
J. B. Banks,	Tax Assessor
J. C. Avera,	County Clerk
J. T. Ferguson,	District Clerk
Joseph Brashear,	Surveyor
Joe Worsham,	Representative
H. C. Connor,	District Judge
R. D. Allen,	District Attorney

Our county is greatly favored with a class of splendid officials, honest, sober, business citizens of the county, every official whose name appears above are citizens of Hopkins County.

The County Commissioners are:

Neal McDonald

W. E. McGill

L. F. Blanset

J. N. Winniford

This body of gentlemen are a practical and shrewd set of business men. They have watched every opportunity that pointed to the business prosperity of the county, and have never failed to avail themselves of it.

VALEDICTORY.

Since we wrote and gave to the public the work entitled "Three Years in a Mad House," grim death has visited our home and removed from earth our dear companion. This sad event has darkened and saddened our life. We will never see her sweet and innocent face again until the morning of eternity breaks open the gates of death and turns the black night of grief and sorrow into everlasting pleasure and never ending sunshine. While this dark and dreary cloud hangs over us like a pall of death, we feel that we must ever drift with the monotonous tide of events, doomed to watch the flowers of hope of our early manhood perish and mingle with the shadows of misfortune and disappointment, When in the midst of care and sorrow, we look far away into heaven's own blue sky, where, we are taught, is the angels' home, we sometimes feel that the storms and tumult of an eventful life have passed away, and the calm that precedes the end of all has come, and in the evening of our day we can look back over the unquiet ocean and the rugged steeps that lie behind, and, Lo! the hours of darkness and storm have gone forever and the sky is shining calmly and serenely down upon us.

Farewell, until we meet again on yonder pearly shore, beyond death's chilling flood.

E. B. F.

THE END.

Index

www.ingramcontent.com/pod-product-compliance
Lightning Source LLC
Chambersburg PA
CBHW021908020426
42334CB00013B/515